Successful Supervision

SECOND EDITION

Successful Supervision

SECOND EDITION

James R. H. White

Drawings by Bernard McCabe MSIA

McGRAW-HILL Book Company (UK) Limited

London · New York · St Louis · San Francisco · Auckland · Bogotá
Guatemala · Hamburg · Johannesburg · Lisbon · Madrid · Mexico
Montreal · New Delhi · Panama · Paris · San Juan · São Paulo · Singapore
Sydney · Tokyo · Toronto

Published by
McGRAW-HILL Book Company (UK) Limited
MAIDENHEAD · BERKSHIRE · ENGLAND

British Library Cataloguing in Publication Data

White, James R. H.
  Successful supervision. – 2nd ed.
  1. Supervision of employees
  I. Title
  658.3'02   HF5549

  ISBN 0–07–084925–0

Library of Congress Cataloging in Publication Data

White, James R. H. (James Richard Henry)
  Successful supervision.

  Includes index.
  1. Supervision of employees.
  I. Title.
  HF5549.W474   1986   658.3'02   86–2739

  ISBN 0–07–084925–0

12345 WL 89876

Typeset by Oxprint Ltd, Oxford and printed and bound in Great Britain by
Whitstable Litho Limited, Whitstable, Kent

Contents

Preface   ix
Your job and the law   xi
Note on action checklists   xii

1. *Achieving results through people*   1
    Your role as a supervisor—planning, organizing, leading,
    coordinating and controlling—employees' fears—how to
    foster the will to work—knowing the individual—setting
    targets—how to build and motivate a
    team—communication and consultation—setting a good
    example

2. *Removing frustration, monotony and nervous tension*   19
    How to beat frustration—make the job more interesting—
    cut down nervous tension

3. *Selecting staff*   27
    How to define what sort of person you are looking for—job
    specification and employee specification—preparing for
    the interview—asking the right questions in an
    interview—obtaining truthful references

4. *Introducing the new employee*   42
    How to welcome the new person into the team—what the
    new employee needs to know—useful items for you to
    know—following through on induction

5. *Your responsibility for training*   50
    How to develop your own ability—taking advantage of
    opportunities—identifying the training you need—
    training subordinate supervisors—delegation, deputizing,
    project work, committee assignments, guided experience,
    job rotation—training non-supervisory staff—helping
    people to learn: successful job instruction—how to make
    individual and section training plans

6. *Group training techniques*   71
    Preparing your material—overcoming nerves—using
    visual aids—the lecture technique—group instruction

7. *Understanding complaints and grievances*   81
    The difference between a complaint and a grievance—
    grievances in disguise—five rules for grievance
    interviews—know your company's grievance procedure

8. *Introducing changes*   89
    Why people may resist change—how you can win them
    over—telling them in advance and consulting them about
    the new arrangements

9. *Reducing disciplinary problems*   99
    How to create the right environment—setting an
    example—knowing your ground—how to put somebody
    on the right lines without arousing resentment—the
    two-stage interview—know your company's disciplinary
    procedure

10. *Your responsibility for communication*   113
    Dinosaur Ltd—the need to relay information both
    ways—how to communicate with your staff—and with
    your boss—what each needs to know

11. *The supervisor's responsibility for safety*   123
     How to promote safety—your legal responsibility—
     promoting safety—planning safety into the job—
     procedure for correcting unsafe employees—older
     employees—young people—the accident-prone

12. *Your union representative and you*   139
     What unions are for—the union representative's job—
     how to work effectively together—the need for courtesy—
     the steward's role when you reprimand an employee—
     know the law, the union and the procedures—don't
     delegate supervisory jobs to the union representative

13. *Don't do it all yourself*   146
     Delegating duties—letting others make decisions—you
     carry the can—thirteen steps to better delegation

14. *The organization: working as a member of the management
     team*   156
     The structure of the organization—the role of
     shareholders, directors, managers, supervisors and
     operatives—line organization—functional supervision—
     line and staff—authority and responsibility—how to
     recognize organizational problems which could be making
     things difficult for you—project teams and matrix
     organization—interdepartmental liaison—how to be
     assertive without being aggressive in communicating with
     other departments

15. *What you can do to improve work methods*   174
     The six steps of method improvement—the questioning
     technique—Quality Circles

16. *Cost reduction*   180
     Cost reduction for all supervisors—budgeting—what is
     meant by productivity—the need to cut costs—six ideas
     for improving productivity—value analysis—cost

reduction for factory production supervisors—machine paced jobs with slack—down-time—make sure that staff report waiting time—cut down on unnecessary work and rework—some useful cost accounting terms—labour costs—direct and indirect—material costs—variable and fixed overheads—standard costing procedure—break even—quiz on cost terms

17. *Planning and managing your time*   200
Are you a tram, bus, or taxi?—key results areas—Pareto and the vital 20 per cent—the need to make time for planning—organizing your desk—the schedule of pending jobs—urgent or important?—keeping a time log and asking the right questions—systems for dealing with recurring jobs—check lists—planning the big job— critical path technique—develop the right habits—the rush job

18. *Using initiative when work is delegated to you*   223
Completed staff work—preventive and contingency plans—creative thinking

19. *Employee counselling*   229
Why counsel staff?—the employee's needs—how to prepare for and conduct a job review interview—a four-point plan—the art of listening—asking the right questions—reflecting—other opportunities for counselling—the sickness self-certification interview

20. *Supervision in the office*   241
Essentials in office supervision—the office supervisor—choosing and training the right people— looking after health and safety—health and safety in the electronic office—securing economy, efficiency and effectiveness—introducing information technology—self development

Index   254

Preface

The duties of a supervisor will depend to a great extent on the kind of business he or she is in, but basically the necessary knowledge can be put under two headings: *technical aspects* and *supervision*. This book deals exclusively with supervision.

It is designed to help section and department heads, whether they are controlling production processes, construction projects, service units, computer teams, or office work, to manage their jobs more effectively and be better team leaders.

Managers, training directors and tutors will also find it extremely useful as a textbook to be used in conjunction with other methods of supervisory training. Staff who are intending to take examinations leading to the NEBSS Certificate or the Institute of Supervisory Management's Certificate in Supervisory Studies should be encouraged to answer the questions at the end of the chapters.

The chapter on supervision in the office has been contributed by Gillian Grenfell, MA, MBIM, Manager of the Business Advice Centre in Leicester. Office supervisors should read this chapter first so that they can see the rest of the book in perspective.

The ideas contained here owe much to the many supervisors, managers and directors from industry, commerce and local government who have discussed their jobs with me, especially my former colleagues from Shell International and The Industrial Society.

I am grateful to Mr Bernard McCabe, MSIA, for illustrating the book so well, and conveying the exact message with his excellent illustrations, and to Mrs Sandra Sargent and Mrs Margaret Shepherd for their application in producing the manuscript.

Your job and the law

In the last few years there has been a marked increase in the number of laws governing the employment of staff, and this trend looks like continuing. Books on industrial relations law seem to be out of date before they come off the press these days, so I shall not describe the current position here, but you have to be alert to the legal applications of what you do as head of your section or department.

The following general principles are unlikely to change:

1. When staff are recruited they are entitled to receive certain information about their terms and conditions of employment.
2. During the period of their employment the law affords some degree of protection against unreasonable working conditions, industrial disease and accidents.
3. Dismissals have to be handled carefully according to certain legal requirements which are based on the concept that an employee's job is a possession which must not be taken away unless the employee is seriously at fault, and if this should happen he or she is entitled to some compensation for the loss of it.

So if you have to engage staff, make anyone redundant, discipline them, or dismiss for misconduct you must bear this in mind as well as the provisions relating to safety, injury, health and welfare. As you know, special rules apply to the employment and remuneration of women, and sex and race discrimination.

If you are ever in doubt about the current position on this or any other point of law and your company does not employ a personnel officer, suggest to your manager that you should seek the advice of the Advisory, Conciliation, and Arbitration Service. Their staff are most helpful and besides giving advice they will recommend to you the most up-to-date explanatory booklets on the point in question.

Keep your eyes open for announcements in the press concerning new legislation and ask your personnel department (or whoever does that job) for the latest booklets which might have a bearing on industrial relations in your department.

Note on action checklists

This book is called *Successful Supervision* because it is designed to help you regularly examine your own performance and see where you could do better.

Ask your manager to go through some of the checklists with you, giving a tick where you both think you are OK and a cross where attention is needed. This will give you a clearer understanding of your priorities and targets for improvement. If your manager considers that an important and sometimes overlooked point should be added to the checklist, be sure to include that in your action plan as well.

Ask a few months later how you have been doing. Some managers are too busy or just too cautious to give you this vital information unless you ask for it.

1. *Achieving results through people*

Your role as a supervisor

As a supervisor you are a first line manager, which means that a significant part of your job is making the most effective use of your resources: manpower, machinery, materials, space and time—in fact money in all its forms. Whatever kind of work you supervise, whether it is in production, distribution, services, maintenance, stores, the office, etc., your job has much in common with the work of other first line managers. Supervisory jobs are like triangles all on the same base line representing those responsibilities which are common to them all (such as planning, leadership, safety and communication). The apexes of the triangles represent those parts of the job which are

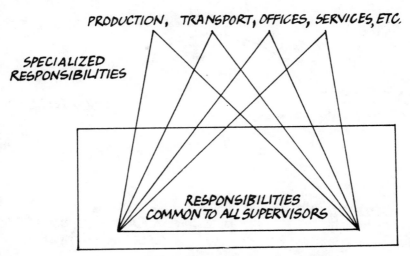

Figure 1.1 The triangular nature of supervisory jobs

different and so require knowledge, experience, and skills peculiar to your trade or profession—such as the tachograph if you are a transport supervisor.

There are five phases of supervision, as shown in Fig. 1.2. So, for example, a building foreman would need to *plan* the construction operation, *organize* the workforce by allocating responsibilities, *lead* them (looking after their safety, health, welfare, and motivation), *coordinate* them (such as making sure that when the concrete arrives on site everybody is ready for it) and continuously *control* what is going on (progress, quality, costs, security, site tidiness, etc.).

Each of your responsibilities involves all five of these phases. For instance, if we take your responsibility for safety, you have to *plan* for safety, *organize* your team with accident prevention in mind, *lead* (motivate people to work safely), *coordinate*, so that they do not endanger each other, and *control* by maintaining good housekeeping and other accident prevention measures.

When you are doing one of these five things (POLCC— remember it by thinking of the POLKA) you are *managing*. When you are doing anything else you are using yourself as a

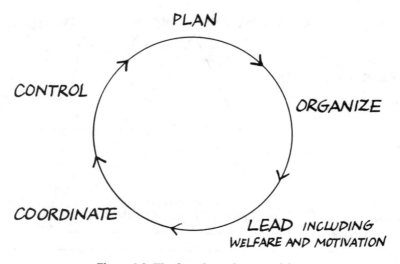

Figure 1.2 The five phases in supervision

unit of labour. Your main priority is to manage, so make sure that you attend to POLCC functions first to enable your team to get on with the job.

You can visualize this balance between managing and doing the work if you think of a piston in a cylinder (see Fig. 1.3).

Every supervisor achieves results through other people and depends on them for success. Staff must first be selected wisely according to the kind of work for which they are needed, and then trained to do it well. The techniques of selection and training which are explained in later chapters will help you if your company expects you to play a part in this process.

When your staff have been recruited and started their training, how do you encourage them to give of their best to their work? The first essential is to identify the reasons why people deliberately restrict their output, and to find ways of removing these causes. Once this is done, it is important to see how, in a group which has no reason not to work, a positive creative drive can be fostered.

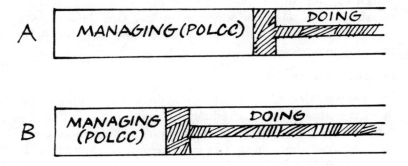

Figure 1.3 In the top diagram the supervisor is allowing enough time to manage but in the lower one he or she is doing too much other work and the management part of the job is suffering as a result

Why do people restrict their output?

Apart from go-slow and work-to-rule orders being used against management openly to force their hand, there are three main reasons why people restrict their output. They all stem from insecurity, and their remedy is only partly in your hands. When you see them operating you should first do what you can within the limits of your authority to remove them, and then advise senior management on any further remedial action you suggest might be taken.

Fear of running short of work

Staff like to see that there is plenty of work coming along to keep them busy during the day and if there is not much to do they go slow to make it last. They may want to ensure the need for overtime if their life style depends upon extra money.

You can temporarily reduce the fear of running short of work by reassuring them about the forward order position, but be warned about the dangers of regular overtime. It is a difficult habit to break.

Through good forward planning you can maintain a steady workload, and you should have some fill-in jobs up your sleeve to take care of slack periods, perhaps preparing for the next peak period, sorting out systems, or getting some flexibility training under way.

Fear of redundancy

Five people will hold back from doing the work of six if it means that the sixth will be made redundant, so it is important to plan your manpower requirements in advance. The company may have to carry redundant staff for short periods pending vacancies arising elsewhere in the organization rather than sack staff and then a few weeks later have to recruit more. Handling redundancies in close consultation with the people likely to be affected, and the use of 'natural wastage', early retirement, or voluntary redundancy with good terms, will all help to reduce employees' fears and combat restrictive practices which have been adopted through the fear of redundancy.

Fear that piece rates may be cut

For certain kinds of jobs, piecework is an appropriate form of incentive. The rates, whether arrived at by time study or by guesswork, tend to slacken when people find short cuts. But instead of the company and the operator both benefiting from increased experience neither does because the operator is careful not to work to capacity in case the rates are revised. Improved rate-setting is partly the answer but it is also necessary to reassure staff that rates will not be revised unless there is a change of method.

How to foster the will to work

So far I have talked about trying to remove the deterrents which make people hold back their full potential. Once this has been done, how do we get them to put quality, effort and enthusiasm into their work?

The key to this is to ask yourself what you as an employee want from your job, and the list will probably include these items:

- a good salary,
- security,
- job satisfaction (seeing good results without too much frustration),
- an interesting job,
- a challenge,
- a good team spirit, cooperation,
- dignity—respect from fellow employees and fellow citizens,
- comfortable and safe working conditions,
- a chance to use your brains and talents,
- a hearing for your complaints,
- reasonable leisure,
- the opportunity to learn and progress.

People's priorities vary, of course, according to their age, sex, family commitments, experience and personality, so if you know your staff as individuals you can strike the right note with each one. For example, a 16-year-old girl would probably not be impressed by the firm's pension scheme—but status, team spirit and good prospects will probably be just what she wants.

A skilful supervisor can anticipate and avoid a grievance by spotting where a person's needs are not being satisfied at work, and sometimes either move that person or change the job content. The industrial psychologist Herzberg points out that removing dissatisfaction in this way is an important step *towards* motivating people, but it will not in itself make people work with greater enthusiasm. To do this you have to provide the opportunity to achieve something—either as an individual or better still as a member of a team—because this will make the individual want to win the approval of colleagues. So make your employees feel important. Treating somebody as second class never gets you first class results.

Get to know the individual employee

The best supervisors never treat their teams as a sea of faces. Knowing their names is a first step. It is a good idea to have a small notebook with two pages for each person in your team, recording personal information as shown in Table 1.1.

Give people something to aim for

We all do a better job when we are given an aim. This target should be reasonably challenging, but not impossible, and we need to see how well we are doing at every stage of progress towards it.

The same psychology can be applied at all levels. The supervisor's targets are the completion of production batches, the meeting of delivery deadlines, completing maintenance schedules, and so on. The clerks, operators, craftsmen and technicians, whose efforts achieve these results, need to see their own goals clearly and feel they are making progress towards them. People's results vary in direct proportion to management's interest in their performance.

Table 1.1 Employee information record

Name ....*Mr/Mrs/Miss*

Address ....

Tel. no ....

Date of birth ....

        (perhaps you won't send birthday cards, but it's a good idea to recognize that day unless the person is deliberately trying to ignore it!)

Date joined company ....

Training received/qualifications ....

....

....

....

Experience ....

....

....

....

Special skills ....

....

....

Family ....

Hobbies/sports ....

....

Notes   Under this heading you can record special information such as health problems affecting the sort of work to allocate or avoid, job likes and dislikes, and perhaps religion if this is a strong influence. You can also record any counselling you have given as to quality of work, safety, etc., together with the date it was discussed.

GIVE PEOPLE SOMETHING TO AIM FOR

Show appreciation

We all like to have someone take an interest in what we are doing and how we are getting on with the job. Some people think that to show appreciation is unnecessary. You know the way it goes:

WIFE: Did you like your dinner?

HUSBAND (*from behind newspaper*): My what, dear? . . . dinner? Oh, all right.

Most of us would rather have constructive criticism than complete indifference, but criticism, too, can be a cumulative poison. Sincere appreciation works best. These days people do not often have responsibility for a complete job—like, say making a piece of furniture, or forging a horseshoe. The master-piece of which you could say 'all my own work' used itself to confer on its maker a mark of appreciation and encouragement. But today, when nobody has the full responsibility for a job, nobody gets the complete satisfaction of finishing it. You can make up for this deficiency by being sincerely appreciative. If your boss praises you for something one of your team has achieved, see that the employee gets the credit for it.

Help to build a team

It is important to understand something about the psychology of group behaviour so that you can build a team. Many of our most profound needs are met by belonging to a group. We suffer without team support, or if we are forced into groups which do not share our values. Groups have great power over their members, and people will sacrifice money, or sometimes the approval of society as a whole, if they have to choose between these and acceptance by their fellows.

A group, of whatever kind—sports club, gang, social clique, or working team—has three main functions:

- to do something in common;
- to maintain itself (it has a will to survive);
- to satisfy the needs of its members.

As a supervisor you can make use of these forces among your own staff in the following ways:

Emphasize the common interest shared by them and the company. Make WORK the group's objective

Ensure that everybody knows how important their product or service is, and what their section's goals are. You have to show real enthusiasm if you expect them to be keen. When you present a group of people with a challenging and worthwhile aim, it is easier to motivate them and keep them on the correct path.

Look after the group

Understand the needs of the group, safeguard the standards which they consider important, and look after them in ways which they think important.

Plan the work so that members have to depend on each other, and so that the value of each individual's work is clear to the group. This will strengthen loyalties. It is a mistake to try and play one person off against another and rule by division. Any enthusiasm people may have for the job soon dissolves each morning with the prospect of having to work in an unfriendly atmosphere. If you can foster goodwill among staff you will find that they develop a sense of responsibility for the whole section's good, and if one member makes a mistake or is temporarily absent they will put in extra effort to compensate.

A group cannot survive without good communication, so keep them informed about the department's progress and about each other's work. Explain and discuss orders, and listen to their ideas.

Look after the members

Study and look after the people in the group, not just their work. All should see their individual role as difficult but important. Try to organize jobs so that they present an element of challenge.

See that they have the right tools

Good tools enable the work to be done better, more quickly and with the most economical use of skilled manpower. They show staff that management is concerned for the quality of the job and that the person who has to do it matters. Nobody wants to work twice as hard as necessary in order to make up for

SEE THAT THEY HAVE THE RIGHT TOOLS

deficiencies in either the equipment or the environment in which it must be used.

Let them make as many decisions as possible

If the work permits, let people use their own discretion on some of the decisions to be made. This makes the job more interesting and staff will work more conscientiously if they feel they are implementing their own ideas and so proving their own judgement.

Consultation

Besides letting employees use their own discretion on how to do a particular job, make a practice of consulting on wider issues. Because you ask people for an opinion on a matter which affects them or their work, it doesn't follow that you have to be bound by it. You don't have to abide by a majority decision. You are the one who is paid to make the decisions, so if, after weighing up all the pros and cons, you decide that you have to go against a subordinate's advice, you must do so.

Listen to suggestions

Some companies introduce suggestion schemes on the basis that those closest to the job often have a great many useful ideas which could cut costs, improve the products, avoid waste, or make the process easier. Whether or not your company runs a suggestion scheme, show an interest in your employees' ideas and see that they are given a fair trial. Make sure that if they are not workable the originator is told why, and see that credit is given for an idea that *does* work. Money is the most tangible reward for good ideas, but many progressive firms consider they are already paying their people to use their brains, and that ultimately their inventiveness will win them promotion. There obviously should be *some* reward, if not an immediate financial one. Read about Quality Circles in Chapter 15. This is a first-rate idea for tapping shop floor brainpower.

See that they are fairly paid

As Groucho Marx said, 'Money may not be able to buy happiness, but you can make a substantial down payment with it.' So if you consider that any member of your staff is not being paid fairly it is up to you to try to get something done about it. You do not have to reveal that you think a particular salary is inadequate, and most probably you will not have the final word on whether or not a rise is given. But you should get all the facts—what is paid and why you think more is deserved—and tell your superior what you recommend.

Wages should match *ability*, and ability should match the *job*. If one of these three elements is out of line with the other two, whether higher or lower, you can expect trouble (see Table 1.2).

Table 1.2

wage	ability	job	✓
wage			✗
	ability	job	
	ability		✗
wage		job	
		job	✗
wage	ability		

Some managers take the view: 'Why should I bother? I shall only get myself a bad name for being a nuisance. If she isn't satisfied she can take it up with the union and let them have a go at management—they will sort it out.' This kind of attitude builds up distrust between management and the staff, fosters the feeling that to obtain justice you have to fight the company, makes nonsense of all efforts to build a common purpose, and in the long run is of great disservice to the organization.

It is not the union's prerogative to manage, and it does not usually want to. But in some firms it has begun to do so because management has abdicated its responsibility to its employees. Staff think that 'everything we have the union has won for us'.

Set a good example

People in your section will take their cue from your behaviour, attitude to the company, and approach to the job. Your punctuality, neatness, high standards and safety-mindedness speak louder than words and will achieve a great deal more as far as the staff are concerned.

Tell people the reasons for doing a job

When people know the purpose of a job and why it is wanted by tomorrow, or why it is to be of a special quality, they put extra effort into it. Knowing what it is for, they can use their own initiative such as whether to use a certain finish, or what improvisation they could make for the sake of speed. 'Theirs not to reason why' went out with the Charge of the Light Brigade. Once the rush job is finished, make sure it is taken away out of sight even if the urgency has disappeared. It is pretty frustrating to see that your superhuman efforts were wasted and the completed job is just sitting there, ignored.

Help to create and maintain pride in the company

In their book *The Winning Streak* (Weidenfeld & Nicholson 1984), Walter Goldsmith and David Clutterbuck made a study of the factors which put the most successful companies in the country at the top of the league table; one of those elements is pride in the company at all levels. People like to work for an organization whose name is associated with quality.

Supervisors have an important part to play in developing this attitude of mind in their teams. How you speak of the organization, what you say about management, your comments about the company when you are off duty, all go to build up its image in the minds of employees and the public at large. Tell your boss if you don't agree with company policy, but do it in private and let there be no doubt about your loyalty when talking to everybody else.

Helping to project a good image for your company can be carried a stage further. Be sincerely and actively interested in the company as a whole. You are not just there to look after your own department, section or shift without regard for the wider team. Without crossing your wires with colleagues in other departments, or appearing to tell them how to do their jobs, you can look at the broad picture and consider how your activities affect the company as a whole.

Example

A supervisor in a clay pipe factory had charge of several inspectors checking the pipes for cracked ends as they came out of the oven on a conveyor belt. It was a boring job and the inspectors' attention would wander, with the result that 10 per cent of the faults were not picked up. All the pipes, including the defective ones, were transported to the customer who of course rejected the cracked ones and was therefore short of serviceable ones.

The supervisor was not bothered and simply said, 'I don't blame the inspectors. My attention would wander, too. Anyway nothing is lost because the defective pipes are recycled and wastage of material is zero.' This company was trying to keep its share of the market in the face of vigorous efforts from a competitor whose salesmen and quality controllers were by contrast very much on the ball.

What would you do, if you were in the supervisor's position, to reduce the 10 per cent of scrap which slipped through undetected? Do you think that 'nothing was lost'? Why?

Require high standards

Do not tolerate poor work. Customers have a right to expect a good quality product and will take their business elsewhere if it is not provided. Staff like to take pride in what they do, and they know that their security depends on the quality of the goods and services they are providing.

These, in fact, are the guidelines most frequently mentioned by managers and supervisors in discussion on the subject of winning the staff's wholehearted cooperation. They are all based on the obvious but often forgotten facts that we all work better if we are given a worthwhile job to do, and feel that we are being treated like responsible people while we get on with it.

Table 1.3 Check list on leadership

Questions	×✓	Notes
1. Do you take positive steps to do what you can to remove the causes of any deliberate restriction of output?		
2. Do you give people objectives or targets, and show interest in and appreciation of their progress towards them?		
3. Do you show sincere appreciation of people's work?		
4. Do you consciously try to build their self-confidence?		
5. Do you give them the reasons for special jobs?		
6. Do you help to create and maintain a pride in the company?		
7. Do you try to build a team?		
8. Do you expect high standards of performance?		
9. Do you consult them, and keep them involved?		
10. Do you listen to their suggestions?		
11. If a suggestion is unworkable, do you explain to the originator the reason why?		
12. Do you try to see that they are fairly paid?		
13. Do you give them the equipment and facilities they need to do the job?		
14. Do you set a good example in: • timekeeping? • attitude to the job? • attitude to the company? • tidiness? • safety?		

Questions	✗ ✓	Notes
15. Do you know all members of your staff—their background, hobbies, education, training, experience and personality?		
16. Do you listen to their problems when they want you to?		
17. Do you show a contagious enthusiasm?		
18. Do you have daily contact with each member of staff?		
19. Do you back up your staff when they need your support?		
20. Do you allocate the right job to the right person, using everybody's talents to the full?		
21. Do you foster pride in the job?		
22. Do you allocate to each person a special area of expertise and responsibility?		
23. Do you take positive steps to increase job interest?		
24. Do you plan the work carefully to avoid unnecessary effort and to keep them busy?		
25. Do you lead by example?		
26. Do you put pace-setters in with each work group?		
27. Do you try to improve working conditions, hygiene and safety?		
28. Are you careful about the selection and training of subordinate supervisors?		
29. Do you interview people who resign, retire, etc., from your department in order to find out good and bad points about the job and the environment?		

Questions

1. It is claimed that a substantial improvement in productivity could be achieved by encouraging the development of team spirit. Discuss this claim, and show how such a spirit could be developed within an organization.
2. Do you think it is possible to develop powers of leadership? If so, why? If not, why not?
3. Before you can motivate people you may have to remove or reduce any factors which may be making them deliberately go slow or withhold cooperation. What might these factors be?
4. What are the main reasons why people may not be able to achieve the necessary level of performance, and what can you do about these factors?
5. What skills does a supervisor need in order to get the best out of a team?
6. What are the benefits of target setting?
7. When would you use a participative leadership style? Does the autocratic style have its place, and if so, when?

2. *Removing frustration, monotony and nervous tension*

People often put more into a job than the results seem to show. Their efforts go to waste on *frustration*, *monotony*, and *nervous tension*. Spoiled work and abortive effort are sometimes caused by domestic trouble and you cannot do much about that, but you may be able to eliminate some or all of the first three items.

How to beat frustration

Work that you feel is being done needlessly or fruitlessly always requires more effort and leaves you unsatisfied at the end of the day.

Good planning and organizing will avoid unnecessary hold-ups, and it is important to plan sufficiently in advance of the job so that once it is under way staff do not have to be switched from one project to another. If your kind of work requires this type of flexibility make sure that when you select staff you choose people whose attitude of mind and previous experience fit them for it. When you do have to switch priorities, always explain the reasons for doing so, and be tolerant when those affected want to let off steam.

Frustration is sometimes caused by delegating duties which are beyond the ability, experience, or terms of reference of the employee, so make sure that he or she has the necessary skills and sufficient authority to see the job through.

When your staff are frustrated by the system within which they work, the actions or inertia of another department, inefficient lines of communication, or red tape, show them what you can do for them by taking up their case and seeing it through to as satisfactory a conclusion as possible.

Make sure that you see every member of your staff each day—or at least twice a week. Daily contact ensures that you become aware of their problems as they arise and can take early action where necessary. By simply being on hand you will cut their frustration by half.

Some frustration arises from a thwarted desire to progress to a better, more interesting job. It pays to win for your department a reputation as a stepping-stone to better things, so give your staff the opportunity to progress. Put forward the names of your most suitable people when top management is headhunting for the next generation of managers. You should be counting your management output—how many supervisors are you developing? How many managers will look back on their first opportunity and have you to thank for it?

If you respect your staff for the job which they are performing at their present level in the company and see to it that their conditions and job titles are acceptable, one possible source of frustration at least will be removed.

Reducing monotony

Job enrichment or work structuring may be the answer to some monotonous manual or clerical jobs. The idea is to rearrange work so that it will be fit for human beings to perform instead of organizing the job in accordance with the needs of technology and forcing people to fit in with its demands. It amounts to: 'The organization of work, the work situation and the work circumstances being structured in such a way that, while maintaining or improving efficiency, job content accords as closely as possible with the capabilities and ambitions of the individual employee: . . . a total integration of technical, economic, and social aims.'
(N. V. Philips' Gloeilampenfabrieken)

The late Douglas McGregor pointed out in 1960 (*The Human Side of Enterprise*, McGraw-Hill) that under modern conditions of industrial life few people are given the chance to use their brains. He distinguished two sets of beliefs about attitude to work, Theory X and Theory Y. According to Theory Y:

1. Work is as natural to most people as play or rest, and people are not basically lazy. Under the right conditions they can enjoy working.
2. Punishment is not the only way of getting them to do the job. They will discipline themselves if they really believe in what the company is trying to do.
3. People will be keen on their work if it is satisfying to them. They will find it so if it gives them a sense of importance and the chance to use their abilities.
4. Under the right conditions most will look for responsibility. When they avoid it, have no ambition, and look only for security, you usually find that this attitude stems from the way they have been treated in the past.
5. Those with imagination, ingenuity and creative talents are not few and far between. Most of the population have these qualities, and every company could make fuller use of its employees' talents in order to guarantee its success and security.

Theory X, on the other hand, assumes that:

1. The average human being dislikes work and will avoid it if possible.
2. Therefore most people have to be forced, threatened, closely supervised and made to get on with the job.
3. Most people prefer to be directed, wish to avoid responsibility, have little ambition, and only want security.

Theory Y questions some of the approaches suggested by work study. Perhaps the scientific solution to a production problem is not always the most effective unless it fully takes into account the human element.

Although you may not be in a position to reorganize working methods except on a small scale and subject to approval from superiors and colleagues, you are likely to achieve better results if you treat people in a way which reflects a belief in Theory Y.

Job interest can be boosted by encouraging training. This helps even manual workers in jobs where there is only slight opportunity for promotion.

Example

In gangs of railway labourers, a few of the supervisors taught the men some facts over and above the details which were strictly necessary. The following figures show that, because it taught them more than the absolute essentials of their present jobs, this training boosted job interest and productivity:

	Percentage of men who said that their supervisor taught them new duties
High-producing gangs	39
Low-producing gangs	19

You can further reduce monotony by showing your interest in a job. The cleaner will put more thought and enthusiasm into dusting the desk and bench tops down if you discuss how important it is to do it well, and what could be done to make the job easier or more effective. Involvement in decision making and discussions with you about the way jobs are done will make employees see themselves individually as an important part of the team.

Where possible, give people extra responsibility. If someone has to fetch and carry a ladder, make that person responsible for checking on its condition and reporting any deterioration, also looking after the key and the padlock which secures it after use. If a clerical assistant has to use stationery, make him or her responsible for maintaining minimum levels, and if possible reordering where necessary.

If you can delegate responsibility according to the particular talents and standards of an employee, you will thus be recognizing that person as an individual and the job will be done with greater enthusiasm.

Your own enthusiasm for the work of the team as a whole will rub off on the members even though they do not go around openly professing it. By being enthusiastic you can stir up interest in even the most monotonous jobs. Table 2.1 shows some guidelines for enriching the content of jobs. You can no doubt adopt some of these ideas in your own department:

Table 2.1

Principle	*Motivators involved*
1. Remove some controls, but retain accountability.	Responsibility and personal achievement.
Example the cleaner draws his own polishes, etc., straight from the store, but has a monthly budget.	
2. Increase the accountability of individuals for their own work.	Responsibility and recognition.
Example the clerk in the pay office has to account to the worker if she has made a mistake. No office supervisor shields her.	
3. Give a person a complete natural unit of work (module, division, area, etc.).	Responsibility, achievement and recognition.
Example a service engineer has his own area.	

Table 2.1 *(continued)*

Principle	*Motivators involved*
4. Grant additional authority to an employee in his activity; promote job freedom.	Responsibility, achievement and recognition.
Example flexible working hours.	
5. Make periodic reports directly available to the individual worker rather than to the supervisor.	Internal recognition.
Example a weaver gets her own loom efficiency % figures daily.	
6. Introduce new and more difficult tasks not previously dealt with.	Growth and learning.
Example operating a more complex machine.	
7. Assign individuals specific or specialized tasks, enabling them to become experts.	Responsibility, growth and advancement.
Example an electrical engineer who shows interest in electronic gadgetry and takes charge of research and development in automation.	

Cut down nervous tension

Nervous tension can develop from unreasonably demanding workloads or from bosses who induce a sense of failure in order to spur people on.

Example

1. A group of women in a dressmaking factory were given an impossible target of 180 dozen garments a day on the assumption that if they aimed at the figure they would not fall far short of it. The work study department knew from their calculations that 140 dozen was about the limit, but the women were not aware of this. When they saw how poorly they seemed to be getting along, their output dropped to under 100 dozen.

   A psychologist who was advising management suggested that a few women should be told the real quota but asked to keep it a secret for the purpose of the experiment. When this was done, the output of those who were in the know increased at once to 120.

2. A similar experiment was performed on some students whose muscular tension was electrically measured while they were doing light work. Half of them were told that they were doing it poorly while the others were praised and given every encouragement. It was found that the 'failure' group were 25 per cent more tense than the 'success' group while working and twice as tense immediately after they had finished the job. Not only had they put more into it but they were not able to relax so well afterwards.

Let them see that they are getting somewhere

Worry, frustration and tension can be reduced if you maintain the sense of progress in your team. Problems are often solved by moving forward instead of worrying about an existing situation. You stay afloat by moving forwards. It is what the business is becoming rather than what it is today which is important, and its managers will be accepted as leaders only if their staff can see that they are going somewhere.

At times every job presents monotony, frustration and nervous tension and we shall never eliminate them completely. But we can reduce their frequency if we recognize the symptoms when staff show signs of strain, consult them on ways of reducing the tension and boredom, and then take all possible steps to stop this waste of energy.

Questions

1. What are the main factors which create nervous tension at work, and how can they be reduced?
2. How might a company improve the job satisfaction of its employees?

3. Selecting staff

A company once decided to buy a machine worth £100 000. There was a careful analysis of its capacity, potential and durability. All those who were going to install it, use it, service it and pay for it had a lengthy conference and at last, after all these deliberations, it was bought and carefully installed. A machine had been selected.

It is ironical that so often a new employee who will spend twenty years with the company and cost in wages and overheads over £300 000 in that time, is selected in ten minutes.

How do you select a person for a job?

There are three stages to go through:

1. Write a *job specification*. (What does the person have to *do* in this job?)
2. Write an *employee specification*. (What does the ideal candidate have to *be*?)
3. Conduct the *interview*.
4. Apply any *tests* which are needed.

You must define the job before you can move on to stage 2 and say what sort of person you will need in order to fill it. When you come to stage 2, the employee specification, consider the items shown on page 31: physical attributes, attainments, intelligence, special aptitudes, interests, disposition, circumstances, availability and age. The following notes will guide your thoughts when doing this.

Duties and responsibilies

Main routine duties.
Special responsibilities for other people, equipment or material.
Commonest difficulties amongst duties or responsibilities.

Working conditions and rewards

Nature of workplace (damp, dirty, noisy, etc.).
Nature of work (heavy, dirty, unvaried, solitary, etc.).
Social opportunities of work (companionship, prestige, team-work, etc.).
What do employees say they like *most* about the work?
What do employees say they like *least* about it?
Anything else to be noted?

Personal characteristics

In drawing up a list of personal characteristics it is important to observe the requirements of the Sex Discrimination Act and the Race Relations Act which prohibit discrimination against applicants on the grounds of their sex, marital status, race or national origin. As long as you consider all applications without prejudice you are free to choose the person you consider to be the most suitable for the job. These are the headings to consider:

Physical Is it important that applicants should be free of any defect of health or physique that may be of occupational importance? Is appearance, bearing or speech important?

Attainments (educational or occupational) What type of education should they have had? How well should they have done educationally? What occupational training and experience should they have had already? How well should they have done occupationally?

General intelligence (upper and lower limits) How much general intelligence should be displayed?

Specialized aptitudes (verbal, manual, mechanical, etc.) Is any marked mechanical aptitude necessary? Manual dexterity?

Facility in the use of words or figures? Special talent or craft skills?

Interests   Would it be useful if applicants showed intellectual, practical, constructional, physically active, social or artistic interests?

Disposition   Should applicants be more acceptable, more influential, more dependable, more self-reliant than most?

Circumstances   What should be an applicant's domestic circumstances (commitments, general background, relationships if important)?

Availability   Can the applicant start when needed?

Age   What are the age limits for the job?

Tables 3.1 and 3.2 show blank forms for stages 1 and 2 and Tables 3.3 and 3.4 show them when completed (a storekeeper's job is used as an example).

After completion of stages 1 and 2, you will be ready for stage 3, which is the interview.

Conducting the interview

Preparation

Look at the application form before you see the candidate. These forms enable you to sort out the non-starters, and you can save everybody's time by saying something like 'Thank you for filling in the form. This job is not cut out for you as it doesn't fit your qualifications. Perhaps we could keep your name on record for one which does?'

If you receive too many unsuitable applicants this means that your advertisement should be more specific about the qualifications needed. By being as detailed as you can in setting out your requirements you will save people's time and trouble.

Table 3.1 Job specification form

Job title:

Duties:

Responsible to:

Supervises:

Other relationships:

    Internal:

    External:

Table 3.2 Employee specification form

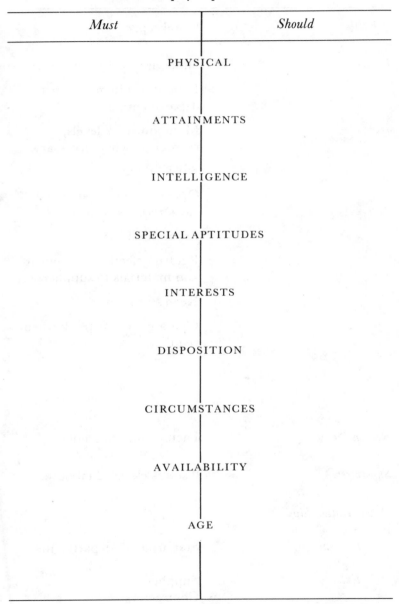

Must	*Should*
PHYSICAL	
ATTAINMENTS	
INTELLIGENCE	
SPECIAL APTITUDES	
INTERESTS	
DISPOSITION	
CIRCUMSTANCES	
AVAILABILITY	
AGE	

Table 3.3 Completed job specification form for storekeeper

Job title:	Storekeeper
Duties:	Supervise stores staff
	Issue stores items against departmental orders
	Maintain stock levels, reordering when necessary
	Stock taking
	Operate the computerized stock records system
	Local purchase
	Return defective equipment and materials to supplier
	Keep store tidy
	Operate fork lift truck when required
Responsible to:	Factory superintendent
Supervises:	2 stores clerks, 2 labourers
Other relationships:	
Internal:	Staff from all departments
External:	Suppliers Contractors

Table 3.4 Completed employee specification form for storekeeper

Must	Should
PHYSICAL	
Good health	
Good hearing	
Not below average physical strength	
ATTAINMENTS	
Some previous storekeeping experience	Storekeeping experience in this industry
Good primary education	Some experience of successful supervision
INTELLIGENCE	
Average commonsense	
SPECIAL APTITUDES	
Experience of computerized stock control	
Good at simple arithmetic	
Clear handwriting	
Orderly way of working	
INTERESTS	
	Mechanical and practical
DISPOSITION	
Helpful and cooperative	
Tactful in supervising staff	
Honest	
CIRCUMSTANCES	
No home circumstances requiring much time off	Not live too far from factory so that he will not be delayed by bad weather, etc.
Own transport or reliable bus service	Stable home background
AVAILABILITY	
Must be available within 3 months	Ideally, available at once
AGE	
21–55	24–45

If the completed application form looks promising, mark your employee specification accordingly. Make a note on the application form so that you can fill in any missing information at the interview and perhaps identify useful leads which would open up the topics you wish to discuss. For example, 'number of children' is a useful lead into the subject of domestic circumstances, if these are relevant.

Notice any unexplained gaps in employment. Has the applicant changed jobs frequently? For example, six job changes or more in ten years is rather a lot, and you should make a point of finding out the reasons. What can you learn from the way the form is filled in about such aspects as intelligence, literacy, and neatness, if these are important for the job?

Find somewhere private for the interview, and try to ensure comfort and freedom from interruptions.

The interview

You want to know all about the applicant so he or she should do nearly all the talking. Put the applicant at ease and prepare an opening remark to break the ice. From the application form perhaps you can find something you have in common. When you have explained the job, its benefits, and the salary, let the applicant talk. Work all subjects round to cover the questions you need answered.

Applicants are often reticent in interviews. Occasionally you will come across the person who does not want the job anyway, and will go away happily if you write 'unsuitable' on the paper from the Department of Employment. Try to spot this candidate early on and terminate the interview.

Assuming that the applicant wants the job but is tonguetied, try to get onto a topic that he or she feels strongly about. A gliding analogy illustrates this point: a glider pilot will attempt to get the aircraft into a 'thermal' of rising warm air which carries the glider up and then gives momentum for a long flight. Hitting on a point which matters to an interviewee is like this. He or she warms to a theme, and gives you some interesting leads. You can spot 'thermals' because the words used will convey feelings such as pride, determination, regret, indignation, etc. Sometimes the intonation of the voice is significant.

An interview might go like this:

APPLICANT (*for garage supervisor's job*): I heard about the job from one of the other parents at the PTA.
INTERVIEWER: PTA?
APPLICANT: Yes, the parent/teachers association at the school. I usually go along there and put a word in once a month.
INTERVIEWER (*sensing a 'thermal'*): What does the PTA do?
APPLICANT: Oh, a lot. Fundraising for the kids' swimming pool. We organized a fete. I'm a pretty keen swimmer myself.

The 'thermal' has given a number of leads:

The applicant has a family.
He cares about his children's education.
Is he involved in other community activities?
Does he take part in organizing them?
What other hobbies has he?
What can we learn about him from these?
As a member of the PTA how does he act? Is he a rebel or an organizer?

Once you get the conversation going you can follow up leads to cover the points on which you need information, such as whether he is a good organizer, what his motivation is, and whether he is constructive in his criticisms of authority. You steer the conversation when you are under way. (It's hard to move the steering wheel if you aren't rolling.)

Here is another example:

APPLICANT: I did quite well at British Products Ltd. A couple of things I did turned out very well there.
INTERVIEWER (*spotting a note of pride*): What were these successes you had?

APPLICANT: Well the first break came when . . .
> (The interviewer just listens, putting in a word of encouragement here and there. Success No. 1 takes about five minutes to describe, discuss and comment approvingly upon.)

INTERVIEWER: You mentioned a couple of successes. What was the other one.

APPLICANT: Yes, the other project was . . .
> (This one is developed in a similar way)

Ask questions to enable the candidate to talk about herself and her interests, but avoid *leading questions*. For example, in interviewing a mechanic you would not say 'Our mechanics have to work pretty hard and spend a lot of time travelling. I take it you won't mind that?' Most applicants will give you the answer you want to hear. Leading questions are a waste of time. A better way of arriving at the information you want is to say 'How demanding was your last job?' 'How many hours did you work each day, or each week, on average?' Questions beginning WHY, HOW or WHAT always invite a more complete answer, because they cannot be answered with a YES or NO.

Here are the sort of questions which will encourage more than one-word answers. Naturally you will use your discretion as to which ones to ask a particular interviewee and at what stage of the interview.

Could you tell me about your career since your left school?
Why are you interested in this kind of work?
What do you see yourself doing in three years' time?
What are your goals in life?
What careers did you contemplate when you were leaving school?
Why do you want to work for us?
Who do you think has most influenced your career?
Which job has given you most satisfaction?
What were the things you liked best about that?
What were the sort of problems you had to deal with?
What did you least like about that job?

What do you think are the attributes of the ideal boss?
Have you ever been in charge of other people?
Why did you leave that job?
Could you tell me about your present job?
What are your main responsibilities?
Could you describe a typical working day?
What do you want from your job?
Does your present job leave you much free time?
How do you like to spend it?
What sort of people does that bring you into contact with?
What have been your main achievements?
What do you think could be done about that problem?
Where do you think things could be improved in your department?
Why do you think that .... happens?
Who do you think should be approached about that?
How can you avoid a recurrence of that .... ?
When do these problems occur?

Follow up

After the interview, sum up the applicant's qualifications and experience, and see whether they match the *employee specification*. Avoid being prejudiced and don't look for somebody who is a replica of the previous holder of the job.

Applying tests

In most jobs there are simple *work tests* which you can set in order to satisfy yourself that the applicant is able to do the job. A secretary could give given some typing and dictation, or a fork lift truck driver could be invited to operate your equipment in the yard.

Besides these, which you yourself can carry out on the spot, there are batteries of tests best left to the specialists, which measure *aptitudes*, *intelligence*, and *personality traits* such as emotional stability or leadership qualities. There is some increase in the use of these, particularly where the investment in training new recruits is expensive and the appointment of misfits would be very costly. If you have been experiencing a high failure rate and turnover among new starters, ask you personnel department whether they could look into this method of grading applicants.

Making your decision, and taking up references

Make up your mind. Is this applicant definitely the person for the job, a possible, or definitely not the right one? Always take up references, especially if you need evidence of particular qualities which a previous employer would be in a position to tell you about.

A telephone conversation with a previous boss will tell you much more than a written reference. Ask the questions listed in the record of telephone references (Table 3.5).

Let the applicant know the result of the interview as soon as possible. Every interview should build good public relations for your company, regardless of the outcome of the application. Sensitivity, consideration, tact and politeness are particularly important in today's climate in which yours may be the twentieth rejection letter the applicant has received this year.

Many companies have a much greater turnover than they realize—probably half the women and a quarter of their men are leaving every year, often as a result of haphazard selection.

Even people in semi-skilled jobs who are recruited, trained and then leave, represent a dead loss of at least £800 to the company. By playing your part in the selection procedure you can save your company a great deal of trouble, inconvenience, and disappointment.

Table 3.5 Record of telephone reference

Name of applicant ....

Position wanted ....

Company name ....

Address ....

....

Contact ....
           (*name*)   (*title*)

Introduce yourself, saying why you are telephoning and what position the candidate is applying for. (The person giving the reference will probably ask for your number and call you back.)

Your pattern of questions could be something like this:

1. When did he or she start and finish his or her employment with you?

   ....

2. What was his or her job? Did he or she change jobs within the organization?

   ....

   ....

3. What position did he or she hold?

   ....

4. How well did he or she work?

   ....

5. What is his or her attitude to hard work?

   ....

6. Did he or she lose any time because of poor health?

                                         YES   NO

   For other reasons?   YES   NO

   Notes: ....

   ....

Table 3.5 (*continued*)

7. What sort of timekeeper was he or she?

8. How did he or she get along with others?

9. How well do you think he or she would fill our post? Would the job conditions and circumstances present any problems for him or her?

10. Why did he or she leave your company?

11. Would you re-employ him or her?   YES   NO
    If not, why not?

12. What are his or her strong points?

    What are his or her weak points?

13. Other information:

Note: Telephone references should only be taken up if the applicant knows and approves.

Table 3.6 Check list on selection procedures

Questions	✗✓	Notes
1. Do you always write a job specification and an employee specification so that you know what kind of person you are looking for?		
2. Do you ask applicants to fill in an application form and make time to study it before the interview?		
3. Do *you* interview people who are going to work for you before the company engages them?		
4. Have you received training in interview techniques?		
5. Do you use aptitude tests whenever possible?		
6. Do you ask the applicant's permission to seek a previous employer's reference, and obtain this on the telephone whenever possible?		

Questions

1. Prepare a job specification and an employee specification for a driver (company light van) who has to deliver goods to customers.
2. Do you think that the immediate superior (section head, supervisor) of the prospective employee should be involved in the selection procedure? Why?

4. *Introducing the new employee*

Induction is the process of assimilating a new employee into the company and helping him or her to become an effective and co-operative producer as soon as possible. New starters may be school leavers or mature people who have worked elsewhere before. Whoever they are the way in which you treat them for the first week will exert a strong influence on whether or not they stay and whether their attitude is one of cooperation or indifference.

How to welcome the new employee into the team

Try to make the person feel at home and interest him or her in the job, the department and the company. Some firms go to considerable trouble to arrange for new employees to be shown around and to demonstrate the part their department plays in manufacturing the final product. Most are convinced that good induction improves teamwork throughout the company.

It is a mistake to think that all that is needed is a talk from the personnel or training officer, or a copy of the employee handbook to read. It is the supervisor who represents the company as far as the new person is concerned, and you are the one who will exert the biggest single influence on the beginner's attitudes.

As a supervisor you must take an interest in all beginners in your department regardless of whether they have been given the routine reception by personnel department. You yourself do not have to impart all the necessary information to them but you should ensure that somebody does.

DON'T TRY TO TELL HIM TOO MUCH AT ONCE

Many supervisors take new employees to one side on their first day and deal with the following points. They are careful to put across the most important things first and not try to give too much information at once. You may like to use the following checklist next time you welcome a new starter.

What new employees need to know

Company information

Name
Organization
Products—how they are
  made, used and serviced
Customers
Managers' names
Employees
Rules and traditions

Departmental information

What it makes
Where it fits
Jobs
Organization
Supervision—names
Employees
Departmental rules
Breaks: tea, meals

Safety

Reporting accidents
Fire precautions
Safety committee
Safety representatives

Where the job fits in

Personal responsibilities and
  job aims

Pay and hours

Rate: deductions, queries
Pay: when and how
Bonus: production, annual
Hours: overtime, weekends,
  shifts, clocking

Industrial relations

Trade union
The shop steward
Grievance procedure,
  especially the first step
The Works Committee

Services, welfare and amenities

Canteen
Holidays and holiday pay
Sickness: notification,
  self-certification
Requests
Time off
Promotion
Travelling
Pension scheme, if any
Sick club
Savings club
Telephone calls
Further education
Toilets and cloakrooms
Overalls
Protective clothing
Sports/social club

Standards

Efficiency
Quality
Safety
Good housekeeping
Absenteeism
Lateness
Smoking
Cooperation

Discipline

Expectations: what you expect from them, what they can expect from you

Personal relationships

Help and cooperation

Ensure the new starter of your support and help

Encourage the person to come to you with any problems

Point out that the department is a team and cooperation is its watchword

Note: The Contracts of Employment Act requires that within 13 weeks of starting, a full-time employee should be given much of this information in writing, so be sure that this is not overlooked.

Useful items for you to know

The new person's experience, including any evidence of leadership experience.

Where they worked before.

Personal likes and dislikes.

Hobbies and sports.

Family.

Friends and acquaintances in the firm.

Where they live and how they travel to work.

Some people like to keep themselves to themselves, so be tactful and do not go beyond a friendly interest—make it a conversation, not an inquisition.

These points will not all have the same importance. Some *must* be covered, others *should* be if possible, but others may be just background information. Certain items will not apply at all. It is a good idea to grade this information in your mind, so that you do not waste instruction time on items in the third category when you should be ensuring that all first category information has been given.

DO NOT WASTE TIME ON THE OUTER RING UNTIL YOU HAVE DEALT WITH THE BULLSEYE

When you have your talk with the new employee put him or her at their ease and welcome them in a friendly way, with a smile. Tell them what they can call you—some supervisors find it a good idea to get that in before anybody else does. Find out if the person knows anybody in the company, and if you are dealing with a school leaver who has never had a job before, remember that it is difficult making the changeover from school to work because of the totally different circumstances to be found there. Here are just some of the differences:

School	Work
Only six hours a day	36–40 hour week and perhaps three weeks' holiday
Three months' holiday a year	
More variety of activity— different classes, games, etc.	Probably less varied activities
More changes of workplace	Usually in one spot
Companions of same age and outlook	Companions of all ages, not so easy to communicate with
Little danger of accidents	Hazards
Constant development of the individual	Development of the individual not the prime aim
No problem of job security	Job security can never be total

These two lists clearly show that the transition from school to work involves the young person in a drastic readjustment and needs to be handled with consideration on your part.

Whatever the person's age see that the new team member is told everything he or she needs to know. Introduce the newcomer to your deputy and the other team members, not forgetting the union representative if you have one. Many supervisors allocate a special person to look after a new starter; someone who is of the right age and disposition. If you don't already do this, try it.

Where induction ends and job training begins

Induction is the reception of a new member of staff into the company, while training is the sequel—the process of imparting the knowledge and skills needed for the job. Some new starters are already competent and need no training, but others will need instruction. Your company may have a training centre for new entrants and in this case you will have few worries as long as you maintain close cooperation with it. Quite a number of supervisors, however, find that they themselves are responsible for seeing that training is done on the job. Don't just leave the new employee to learn by observing an experienced operator, because this can be a sure way of perpetuating bad habits which have crept in. Experienced operators do not always set the best example, or know how to teach others.

You should talk to each of your people every day, and be available to them, but for the new starter you have to make a special effort to communicate. Make a point of having a special chat with the new starter about two weeks later to allow a settling-in period. By then he or she may have a few small problems to sort out and even if there are none, your interest will be appreciated.

Managers and supervisors who take pains to help new staff to adjust themselves to their new working environment find that their trouble is amply repaid in reduced staff turnover and in improved cooperation. So next time you fill a vacancy, take the opportunity of laying the foundations for a long and mutually profitable partnership between the newcomer and the company by giving systematic, regular, friendly attention.

Table 4.1 Checklist on your induction procedure

Questions	✗✓	Notes
1. Do you have few new people leaving within weeks of joining your department?		
2. Do you spend at least 15 minutes getting to know every new employee?		
3. Do you plan what you are going to tell him or her and ask him or her?		
4. Do new staff tend to settle down quickly in your department, making friends easily?		
5. Have all your staff had the opportunity of going all round the company to see what goes on outside their own part of it?		
6. Does anybody teach a new person the job or do they just 'pick it up'?		

Questions	×✓	Notes
7. Do you make a point of seeing new starters between one and two weeks later to ask if they have any problems?		
8. Do you never find breaches of regulations which have occurred through ignorance?		
9. What special steps do you take to help school leavers to adjust to your department?		
10. What special steps do you take to help newly appointed supervisors to adjust to your department?		
11. Do you ensure that they are given the information required by the Contracts of Employment Act, etc.?		
12. Do you carry out a simplified form of induction procedure for staff who are transferred to your department?		

Questions

1. To what extent do you consider good induction can improve employee relations in the company?
2. To what extent should the supervisor become involved in the induction process?
3. Imagine that you have just started in a new job. Describe your feelings, and what help, advice, information, etc., you would want from your new boss in your first week.

5. *Your responsibility for training*

Since supervisors are responsible for their departments' output, they must also make themselves responsible for the competence and ability of their staff. This means that they must diagnose training needs and make arrangements to satisfy them.

They should be concerned about training:

themselves;
subordinate supervisors;
the non-supervisory staff of their departments.

How to develop your own ability

Your capacity to do your present job depends on what you are expected to achieve and how your abilities measure up to those demands. It is important that you should know what is expected of you, so try to put down on paper the terms of reference of the position you occupy. Then you have to take stock of your knowledge, skill and qualifications and see where, if at all, they fall short of what is needed.

Training to do your present job better is not, however, the only kind of development possible. There are a great many other ways in which you can increase your scope and calibre. A growing number of supervisors are undergoing courses for the Certificate of the National Examinations Board in Supervisory Studies. The syllabus requires 240 hours of education (often with day release, spread over a year). This illustrates the amount of time and effort which many companies consider it reasonable to devote to supervisory development.

The following list of suggestions is intended to provide ideas for improvement in your present job and growth potential for your future career.

1. Reading: Ask to be put on the company's circulation list of trade and technical magazines. The quarterly magazine of the Institute of Supervisory Management contains some very good articles.
   Look for management books in your local library.
2. Join professional bodies in your field.
3. Join management and supervisory discussion groups.
4. Attend courses, seminars, conferences.
5. Obtain the prospectus of your local technical college.
6. Learn all you can from the sales representatives who visit your company on behalf of suppliers of equipment, tools and techniques. Although they are there to sell rather than educate, they do provide valuable leads about the latest development.
7. Watch out for TV and radio programmes on management.
8. Attend a work study appreciation course.
9. Supervisors are going to need the following skills to an increasing degree, and courses are available in all of them:
   - problem analysis and decision making;
   - interviewing (discipline, grievance, advice, selection, appraisal);
   - conducting a meeting (e.g. discussion with subordinates);
   - putting a case or argument.

Take advantage of your company's training and development programme

Show that you are interested. Your chief, the personnel manager and training manager are ready to help those who want to help themselves. Don't be backward in asking for help, or feel that you'll be revealing a secret weakness. One of the necessary qualities of a supervisor is the ability for self-analysis and the determination to improve.

Where can you go for outside help and guidance on suitable courses?

Management Training Consultants,
25 Saint Nicholas Place, Leicester.
Tel. Leicester 27062

The British Association for Commercial & Industrial Education,
16 Park Crescent, London W1N 4AP.
Tel. 01–636–5351

The British Institute of Management,
Management House,
Cottingham Road, Corby, Northants, NN17 1TT.
Tel. Corby 4222

The Industrial Society,
48 Bryanston Square, London W1.
Tel. 01–262–2401

The Institute of Supervisory Management,
22 Bore Street, Lichfield, Staffordshire.
Tel. Lichfield 51346

The National Examination Board for Supervisory Studies,
76 Portland Place, London W1N 4AA.
Tel. 01–580–3050

Your own industry's Industrial Training Board or Training Association.

What subjects are covered in supervisory training programmes?

The following list is almost a complete inventory, and it is therefore unlikely that all items would be relevant to any one supervisor, but it shows you what the field covers.

1. Planning and the effective use of time.
2. Quality control techniques, Quality Circles.
3. Health and safety at work.
4. Instructional techniques.
5. Problem analysis and decision making.

6. Human relations, leadership, team building, motivation, induction, giving orders and directions, correcting and improving employees, handling complaints and grievances, human problems at work (case studies), resistance to change, communication (need for and organizing of) including chain of command (briefing groups) consultation, representative systems, employee opinion surveys, suggestion schemes and mass media. Industrial relations.
7. Systems of payment: individual incentive schemes, group incentive schemes, job evaluation and merit rating.
8. Administration of the job: effective job organization: budgeting time, scheduling work, delegating, planning, critical path or network analysis, records, procedures, systems.
9. Training and employee development: department training, individual training, talent spotting, guiding subordinate supervisors, management succession and career development, problem analysis and decision making.
10. Principles of organization: relationships within an organization—line, staff, functional, lateral, position descriptions and terms of reference, authority and responsibility, delegation and completed staff work, spans of control, unity of command versus functional multiple direction from a team of specialists.
11. The tool subjects: organization and methods/work study, value analysis, the use of statistical controls, etc.
12. Communication skills: report and letter writing, putting a case, talking to groups of people, conducting a meeting, interviewing (for selection, counselling, grievance, performance review, etc.).
13. The use of service departments: management accounting, cost accounting, budgetary and cost control, quality control, production control, personnel, training, industrial engineering, O & M/work study, safety; the structure of this company.
14. Background knowledge/general education: economics, structure of the economy.

Training subordinate supervisors

TRAINING YOUR SUBORDINATE SUPERVISORS

Everything under the previous heading applies to subordinate supervisors (section leaders who are responsible to you), but in addition you need to do the following:

1. Define each supervisor's particular goals and provide the resources necessary for achieving them.
2. Periodically discuss progress towards these goals and give help and guidance where needed.
3. Use the supervisor as the main line of communication to the staff and encourage him or her to come forward with the grievances, questions, and suggestions which subordinates have raised.

4. Regularly call your supervisor(s) in on informative, consultative, and problem-solving meetings. In-company supervisory training sessions can be arranged in order to improve supervisors' understanding of their role in the management team and the functions of other departments.

5. Look at the requirements of the job and the knowledge and skills of the supervisor, and when there is a deficiency provide training to remedy it. If promotion is feasible, the same exercise can be carried out for the next rung of the ladder.

6. Examine the contents of any training course intended for the supervisor, briefing before and debriefing afterwards so that the relevance of the course to the job is clarified.

7. Constantly create situations which call for and encourage learning. These include delegation, understudying, project work, committee assignments, Quality Circle leadership, guided experience, and planned job rotation.

Delegation

This means allowing people to take decisions and use discretion on your behalf. The chapter entitled 'Don't do it all yourself' gives you guidelines on how to go about this. Delegation allows people to make decisions and take responsibility, exercising their knowledge and skill and making them want to learn more so that they can handle these situations.

Understudying

Allow different section leaders or potential supervisors to take over from you when you are away. If you give two or three this opportunity, no one person will take it for granted that he or she is automatically in line for your job. This keeps several people on their toes, and avoids anyone building up hopes which may not be realized.

Project work

You can set projects for your section leaders which will help you to achieve your own targets and at the same time give them valuable experience.

Here are some projects which have been assigned to staff with this in mind:

Training Submit a training schedule to ensure sufficient trained staff to give adequate coverage of all jobs in the event of sickness.

Safety Work out an inspection schedule to cover all danger points. Prepare a safety talk for the operators in the department.

Cost control Study the waste problem and make recommendations.

Quality Circles Find out about Quality Circles and submit your recommendations to your department head.

Stores Work out a better stock control and recording system.

It is most important that project work assigned as a method of staff development should in fact be properly completed and the end product *utilized*. Frustration and resentment can build up if the hard work put into a project is disregarded or shelved.

Committee assignments

Encourage subordinate supervisors to sit on committees dealing with safety, welfare, industrial relations, etc. Ask whether the section leader can accompany you when the boss calls a meeting.

Guided experience

Take a particular weakness of one of your subordinates, diagnose the cause and deliberately plan together how to provide training and experience which will eliminate the defect.

For example, there may be carelessness in filling in some of the information on production control documents. You identify this as a failure to realize its importance; and a half day in the production control office trying to read illegible writing or guess at missing facts will make for more care in the future.

Job rotation

This means allowing a section head to take charge of another section while someone else looks after his own. This kind of sideways move should not occur too often, and it is not advisable to switch people around unless they are going to benefit from it (e.g., if they are in line for promotion and will need broad experience).

Job rotation is helpful in some ways, but presents problems unless done carefully. It has advantages and limitations which you should bear in mind before adopting it.

Advantages of job rotation

1. Rotation broadens an individual's experience.
2. It tests staff by exposing them to different problems.
3. It gives new challenges and interest to people who may be in a rut.
4. It brings new brains to old jobs. A person probably runs out of improvement ideas after a few years in a job.
5. It brings in outside experience.
6. Rotation keeps interest alive when there are no immediate prospects of advancement.
7. Staff can try several jobs and find their true niche.

Limitations of job rotation

1. Rotations upset routine. The job could be jeopardized by transferring a successful employee and trying one who is an unknown quantity.
2. Change can be a bore, too.
3. Top management must ensure that everybody understands what is going on, otherwise staff will become insecure and lose confidence in themselves, thinking they have failed and are being pushed aside.

4. Employees may become insecure if their bosses are playing musical chairs.
5. It is important that the previous supervisor's deputy should be competent technically and practically if the new boss is not experienced in the department's work.

The benefits of conducting briefing groups (departmental meetings)

1. They give out information.
2. They explain reasons for changes, policies, etc.
3. They make clear who is responsible for what.
4. They encourage analytical thought.
5. They create a sense of involvement (team).
6. They give staff a sense of status.
7. Staff learn your way of thinking.

The benefits of the morning inspection

1. It identifies problems, personal and production, so that people can get on with the job.
2. It settles people down to work.
3. It enables you to give a word of encouragement or praise.
4. It maintains standards of safety, good housekeeping, quality.
5. It enables you to spot potential bottlenecks, such as staff shortages and machine breakdowns.
6. It provides an opportunity to reinforce the authority of your deputy.

Training non-supervisory staff

Most supervisors have their share of novices to guide along the right lines, or staff with experience elsewhere who must be instructed in the company's special work methods. If you ensure that your staff are well trained you will find that there is less turnover, waste and injury, greater efficiency and the improved morale which comes of knowing the job and knowing that the supervisor is interested in one's ability to do it. Whether or not you are expected to do the teaching yourself it is important for you to understand the main principles of instructing, because you can then either act as tutor or delegate the job of teaching while knowing how to ensure that it is properly carried out.

Supervisors sometimes fail in their responsibility for training operators. The most common mistake is to leave an employee to learn a job by observing somebody else. Another is to put the trainee with the wrong sort of tutor, somebody who is perhaps very good at the job, but either has no idea how to explain it to somebody else, or may know, but has no inclination to communicate.

Some supervisors are unaware of the problems of learning and will write people off as hopeless if they do not pick up the job very quickly. In fact, they may be quite intelligent but may not learn the knack at once; an immigrant may find inadequate knowledge of the language an obstacle.

It helps to remember that:

TEACHING = HELPING PEOPLE TO LEARN

This statement looks obvious and yet many people pride themselves on having given a very fine lesson regardless of whether the pupil derived any benefit from it. The emphasis in teaching must be put in the right place; it is how much the learner learns that really matters, not how much knowledge the teacher propagates. The Training Within Industry people expressed it in this way: 'If the pupil hasn't learnt the teacher hasn't taught.'

Helping people to learn: successful job instruction

There are eight principles which can be applied in nearly every case when there is teaching to be done. They have proved their validity over and over again by helping people to learn more quickly and more completely a wide range of different jobs. For convenience we will suppose that you are doing the teaching, although in practice you will probably often delegate the job to somebody else. (If you do, why not lend the trainer this book to read up these tips?)

Stimulate the learner's interest

The instructor's attitude counts. Even the dullest routine can be made more interesting with a spark of imagination.

It is up to you to find out what is the mainspring of the newcomer's interest in the job, so that you can use its power from the very start. Earning power usually ranks very high but don't overlook the less apparent but no less important reasons —pride in the finished article, job satisfaction, and the need that most of us feel to be good at what we do. Perhaps the newcomer does not realize the full scope of what can be achieved through the skill that is going to be acquired. It is important to encourage enthusiasm from the start. Know your newcomers and understand their aims, so that you can tie them in with achievable objectives.

Sustain the learner's interest

It is commonly observed among people learning something new that their interest tends to flag after the first three or four attempts. Partly this is because they could make great progress at the start but now their rate of learning appears to be slowing down. They have probably reached the stage of sheer hard work, uninteresting practice, memorizing. There may even be a sense of slipping back—of being less skilful at the beginning of this lesson than they were at the end of the last one.

This stage, which is well known and recognized by education psychologists, is sometimes called a *learning plateau*—a point where progress up the mountain seems to have levelled off. A feeling of frustration may set in unless a sense of progress can be maintained—and this of course is true at every stage of learning. To achieve a sense of progress a learner needs a target: so much to be learned by such and such a date and clear signs that the target is getting closer.

These signs will depend on what you are teaching. They may

be in the form of progress through the instruction manual, periodic trial runs, or being entrusted with progressively more challenging exercises. Your interest will stimulate the trainee's enthusiasm.

It has been found that most people respond best when they earn approval for a good performance or incur criticism for a bad one. When the instructor says nothing either way, for a long time, they tend to lose interest.

Build self-confidence and confidence in you

Self-confidence:

- Show that you know she can do it. A battle is half won if you think you can win.
- Handle his mistakes properly. If he gives the wrong answer to your questions try to see why he answered in that way. If part of his thinking was correct give him credit for that part when pointing out his mistake.
- Keep your temper. If you get angry your pupil will become flustered and nervous, try too hard and make more mistakes.
- Give her credit for what knowledge she already has. She may already know a little about your subject and it probably seems quite a lot to her. Many instructors classify such people as know-alls, and try to convince them that they don't know as much as they think they do. This can be very damaging to the learner's morale and quite confusing, unless the existing knowledge is reconciled with what you are telling her. It is hard sometimes to resist telling a trainee that what she learns on day-release is all right in theory but doesn't work in practice. Be patient and try to explain why this is so.

Confidence in you:

- Aim at the highest standards. Nobody wants to put in an extra effort if the outcome is only going to be a sloppy second-rate performance.
- Show the learner that you know your subject.

DON'T GET ANGRY IF HE MAKES MISTAKES

- Show that you have patience.
- Show that you have a systematic plan for teaching and that you are using it.

Prepare your instruction in advance

What you need to say   Decide on the priorities. In any subject there are sections which it is vital for the learner to know—facts without which there can be no understanding of the subject at all. These can be called primary items. There are also secondary items which you would like to explain, incidental pieces of information which are not essential. Make sure that if time is limited you do not miss out the essential facts through spending time on the secondary ones.

Break the job into steps. Ask yourself: what do I do first? Then, what comes next? and so on until you have the job broken down into separate stages, none of them so long that the learner has difficulty in remembering. A good example can be found in the telephone kiosk where dialling instructions are given like this:

Have your money ready.
Lift the telephone.
Dial when you hear the dialling tone.
When you hear rapid pips put a coin in.
Speak.

Teaching aids Make sure that you have close at hand any tools or instruments, books or illustrations which you will need to use for demonstration.

Let the newcomer have a try under your guidance

The trial run is a very important part of the learning process because it consolidates understanding and provides you with an opportunity to spot and correct mistakes. Sometimes it helps to ask them to give a running commentary as they are doing the job. Continue with as many trial runs as you consider necessary.

For safety's sake, do everything possible to remove from the job any causes of potential accidents.

When you teach, tell and show

It has been proved by experiment that when you *tell* and *show* people how to do a new job this is very much more effective than when you just tell or just show. Telling is not enough: it is important to show the acting pilot officer which is the ejection seat button, not just to tell him. Showing is not enough: nobody would sit a learner next to a concert pianist and expect him or her to learn by observation how to play the instrument. The machinery in your department can be just as baffling to the novice, so remember that besides seeing and practising there must be a proper explanation.

Ask questions so that you can be sure you have been understood

There are two levels of technical learning. A trainee can be shown how to perform a certain sequence of actions which will give an end result, and yet never understand how the result is achieved. This is the shallower level of learning and it does enable the person to cope with events as long as everything goes smoothly. The deeper level of learning combines understanding and memory together so that the learner understands the underlying principle, sees through the job and can even improvise if things go wrong.

Whenever somebody needs to have this second type of knowledge, which one might call *insight*, you should ask questions during or after the trial run stage. You might ask 'Why do you think this happens? How do you think it works? or 'What do you think would happen if such and such a step were missed out?' These questions leading into a discussion will develop real understanding.

Revise

How soon do people forget what they learn? Research has shown that one hour after a lesson, people are likely to forget over half of what they learned during it. The following table tells you more about how much people tend to forget:

Time interval since learning	% forgotten
20 minutes	42
1 hour	56
8 hours	64
1 day	66
2 days	72
6 days	75

We know that the learner has constantly to be reminded of the important things or they will be forgotten. Many instructors surmount this problem by assigning certain exercises to be carried out whenever time permits. If you are unable to do this, make a time allowance at the beginning of your second lesson to go over again the main points to be recalled from the first.

Practice

The most effective sort of revision is practice on the job, so give the learner as much opportunity as you can to exercise newly-acquired skills and knowledge by practising solo.

Make a training plan for individuals

Ideally every employee's training need should be analysed by specifying what should be known, what is known, and therefore what still has to be learnt. This may be too large a task to tackle in the short term so begin with your key personnel, those whose jobs are critical to the quality and speed of the department's work.

If you look at the individual training needs analysis form on page 66 you will see how to specify the item which the employee has to know or do. Then there is a column for whether knowledge and ability for each item is adequate or improvable and then a third column for specifying training needs.

Table 5.2 shows an individual employee training schedule sheet, which is the sequel to the analysis mentioned above. On it you can schedule the target date for whatever training you have prescribed, and also note down where and how the trainee is going to be given the required instruction.

Make a training plan for the department

Suppose that, as happens in many departments, a supervisor has a certain number of staff and a certain number of jobs and requires everyone to be trained so that they are versatile

Table 5.1 Individual training needs analysis (for present job)

Name ....

Job title ....

Responsible to ....

Supervises ....

1. DUTIES (general description of the scope of his responsibilities)

2. SPECIFIC DUTIES ITEM	Adequate	Improvable	TRAINING NEEDED

Table 5.2 Individual employee training schedule

Name ....

Job title ....

Responsible to ....

Training items	Target dates	Comments

enough to tackle several kinds of work, thus covering the department in case of sickness, resignation, or a special rush job requiring an all-out effort by everybody.

One way of planning a training timetable is to square off a sheet of paper as in Table 5.3 showing jobs along the top and employees down the side.

Tick off who can do which jobs and this will show you at a glance those operations for which you are short of trained staff. The next step is to mark in your plan the date by which you want to train each person, bearing in mind who is leaving, who are the least versatile and ought to be trained first, and what the future workload is going to be. The letter 'T' and a date shows that, for example, Hill must be trained in coding by November 15, to take over from Brown who is leaving. Some trade unions under certain circumstances may not want to go along with having full interchangeability between jobs, so point out the advantages to staff, such as security, pay and so on, and at the same time try to meet the union's objections. Sell the idea to the workforce and they will influence their representatives.

Table 5.3 Stores administration section training plan

Dept: Stores Section: Admin	Invoices	Coding	Inventory	Issues	Remarks
Brown	√	√	√	√	Leaving firm 30/Nov.
Hill	√	T 15/Nov.		√	
Charles	T 30/Nov.		T 30/Nov.	√	
Cross			T 15/Nov.	T 15/Dec.	
Smith	T 7/Nov.	T 30/Nov.	T 15/Dec.		Joins firm 1/Nov.
Notes on workload			Stock-taking Dec.		

There is surely no more practical way of developing good relations in your department than by showing your concern for the staff and their security through the medium of an effective training policy.

Table 5.4 Check list on training

Questions	×✓	Notes
1. Do new recruits quickly become producers?		
2. If you delegate to somebody else the training of members of your team, do you continue to show interest in their progress?		
3. Have you a training plan for your successor and is it being followed?		
4. In the absence of any one of your employees, is there someone capable of doing that job?		
5. Are people in your section capable of doing more then one job?		
6. Do your experienced staff know how to instruct?		
7. Do you know how to instruct?		
8. Do you prepare a job breakdown (very simple instruction manual) for the jobs you most frequently have to teach?		
9. Has your department a good safety record?		
10. Does your department use materials economically (therefore skilfully)?		
11. Do you analyse people's mistakes with them in an encouraging way?		
12. Does the department continue to function smoothly in your absence?		
13. Are all of your long-service staff keeping up with the times?		

Questions

1. Some supervisors assume that a new and inexperienced employee sitting next to an old hand ought to be able to learn the job through observation. How successful is this method of imparting knowledge and how to you think it can be improved upon?
2. What are the benefits of effective training
   (a) to the company,
   (b) to you,
   (c) to the person being trained?
3. 'Training is the training officer's job' is only partly true. Give your comments.

6. Group training techniques

If you are called upon to speak in front of a group of people—either your own team or staff from other departments, this chapter will help you to stimulate and retain their interest and then convey your message to them confidently.

Preparing what you are going to say

Visualize the people you are going to speak to. What do they know already, and what do they need to know? Why do they need this information? If you bear this in mind when you are preparing your talk, their attention will not wander when you come to deliver it.

Arrive at the meeting room early

This will give you time to lay out your paperwork and any visual aids you will be using so that you are calm and in control when you need them.

Overcoming nerves

If you are nervous when speaking to a group, that's good news. Nerves are normal, and if you are keyed up it will help you to sparkle as a speaker. You will need that adrenalin to meet the challenge. Here is what to do to keep the butterflies under control:

1. Prepare well so that you know what you are going to say and do.
2. Have a glass of water handy.
3. Take some deep breaths before you speak.

4. Wait until your audience are quiet.
5. Begin your session in a steady unhurried way.
6. Find a friendly face in the audience to start with but then have eye contact with all of them in turn.

Finish your session on time

Don't overrun your time. If you encroach on the next person's slot or extend the end of the session your audience may well start switching off.

NERVES HELP YOU MEET THE CHALLENGE

Using visual aids

Visual aids help to reinforce the spoken word and a diagram, model or illustration may be the only way you can convey certain messages or impressions.

The white board or flip chart

Blackboards are a thing of the past. Dusty, messy, scratchy, difficult to clean, evoking classroom memories, they should now be cleaned, painted black once and for all, and equipped with large spring clips for holding flip chart pads.

The non-porous glossy white board is a better proposition. You write on it with special felt tipped pens which must be of the dry wipe variety otherwise the ink will become indelibly engrained.

The best proposition of all is the flip chart pad mounted on an easel, because:

- it doesn't need cleaning;
- you can flip pages over and refer back to them if need be;
- it looks more professional.

Ensure that your board is well placed, so that everybody can see it, and in a well-lit part of the room. Write in large letters and avoid pale colours such as yellow—even green and orange are difficult enough to read from the back. Try out your letters for size and your crayons or felt tips for clarity by writing them up and then going to the back of the room to see whether they are legible. Crayons are more reliable than felt tips because they do not dry out or squeak.

When using the board, don't write at the same time as you are speaking. It is much more effective if you make your statement first and then turn and write it up, because this gives the group time to assimilate what you are explaining.

If you have something long or complicated to illustrate, it will need some prior planning and you can do this lightly in pencil on the chart paper before the session begins.

WILL THEY BE ABLE TO READ YOUR VISUAL AIDS?

Overhead projector transparencies

For diagrams, graphs, etc., which require careful preparation, the overhead projector is without doubt the best answer. Ask your photocopier suppliers about producing black and white projector slides for diagrams. It is almost as easy as straight-forward photocopying, the important point being to use the right grade of acetate sheet. Alternatively you can draw straight onto the acetate with coloured felt tipped pens, which enables you to produce coloured projections.

Try your slides out while you are producing them so that you are sure they can be seen clearly from the back of the room.

Overhead projectors are usually fitted with removable rolls of acetate film so that when you have used the section which is above the glass you roll on to a clear patch. Writing on the illuminated acetate can be dazzling, so when there is not much writing to be done the flip chart is probably better. In any case always ask for a flip chart as well so that you can vary your visual aids and have a standby arrangement should the projector bulb fail. By the way—have a spare, it's very reassuring!

The lecture technique

The lecture or talk has been criticized as lacking participation and not ensuring feedback or retention. Yet it will always play an important part in training. It is useful for introductory sessions and subjects of general interest, or giving an outline of a new thesis or technique; sometimes it is the only method you can use in the circumstances, such as when you have a large audience.

If you have to deliver your material in lecture form here are some hints on keeping your audience attentive and retentive:

A good lecture involves three stages:

- *Preparation*
- *Presentation*
- *Summary*.

Preparation

It takes at least four times as long to prepare a talk as it does to give it. In your preparation, bear in mind that 30 minutes is probably the maximum time the audience can listen attentively to one speaker. You need to intersperse a longer session than that with discussion, question and answer, a film, or some other element of variety.

Grade your subject matter into the three categories mentioned in the chapter on Induction:

1. Must know.   2. Should know.   3. Nice to know.

Ensure that all category 1 is covered; 2 is optional; 3 is unimportant.

Don't pack too much in.

Plan when you are going to answer questions, and tell your group whether to interrupt or wait until a given time.

Prepare your hand-outs and visual aids.

Even if you have given this talk several times before, you should always read your notes through again before the session to make adjustments for this audience and so keep it fresh.

Your appearance
You are a visual aid! Your appearance, clothes, etc. all add to the general impression so make sure that they convey the right message.

Presentation

Avoid reading your whole talk out from a paper as this stops you from maintaining eye contact with the group. If you are speaking from a text it is a good idea to underline the main points as prompters for yourself and then speak conversationally to your group about them.

The best technique is to note down clearly printed headings and use these as talking points. You will then be able to interact with the audience and your talk will have the added interest of gesture, stance, expression, and personal enthusiasm. You can also receive messages from them.

Arousing interest
Your opening remarks—in fact the first four minutes—are vital. During that time you should make them want to learn, and sit up and take notice.

- You may ask a few challenging questions which you know are on *their* minds.
- Show the continuity of this session with what has gone before.
- Use visual aids.
- Look alive.

Note taking
Let the group know whether they need to take notes or whether you will be giving them pre-printed ones. Some people say that you should give the notes out afterwards but I prefer to give them out before so that they can make notes in the margin.

Question time
It is very important to invite questions as this gives an opportunity to fill in any gaps and lets you know whether your message is coming over clearly. Either invite them to ask questions at any time or stop every ten minutes or so. There is often a deadly silence when you ask whether everything is clear, because people are usually reluctant to appear slow. A good technique at this stage is to tell the group that you would like them to discuss with the person sitting near to them any questions or points they wish to raise. Allow them two or three minutes for these 'buzz groups' to operate and *then* ask for questions and you will receive a lively response.

Summary

How do you wind up your session? It is definitely an anticlimax to gather up your notes and say 'That's about *it*!'

At the end you should *summarize*, highlighting all the main points, and think of something thought-provoking or inspiring to say for the finale!

Group instruction

This technique is used when you have to communicate facts which you want your group to retain completely. Whereas a lecture may be used for imparting a general picture or back-

BUZZ GROUPS LIVEN-UP QUESTION TIME

ground information, group instruction is recommended for conveying facts and ensuring their assimilation. So, for example, if you were talking to a number of supervisors about work study you might use the lecture to give them some examples of what it can do, but you would need to use group instruction to ensure that they remember the meaning of the symbols which are used in methods planning.

Whereas the lecture only involves preparation, presentation and summary, *group instruction* involves five stages:

- Preparation
- Presentation
- Summary
- *Recapitulation*
- *Test*

As I have already mentioned preparation, presentation and summary, which are the same in group instruction as in the lecture, I will confine this part of the chapter to recapitulation and test.

Recapitulation

In the recapitulation, instead of telling your audience over again what you have already said, you give them the mental exercise of recalling this information. So you ask questions, but you request them not to call out the answers, otherwise the lazy ones will not bother to think and will let the eager ones get on with it.

You pose the question, allow everybody a few minutes to think and then choose the group member whom you want to reply. This gives you control over who is going to answer. By the way, don't call out the person's name and then pose the question because everyone else will say 'thank heavens he didn't pick me', and not bother to try and remember.

Distribute your questions.

Prepare them carefully, avoiding questions with too many possible answers, e.g. 'What is the first thing you notice when you go into a well organized company?'

Don't forget to hide the visual aids with all the answers on. If someone gives you the wrong answer, give the correct one unambiguously, without making the person feel like an idiot.

Test

The test will tell you if the group has assimilated what you wanted them to learn. The recapitulation told you that some people knew the answers to *some* questions, but the test finds out exactly how much each person remembers. The main points of your talk should be summarized in question form and the question should be capable of only one answer. For example in asking about the maintenance of a particular vehicle, you might ask:

- What should be the tyre pressure?
- What is the service frequency?
- What octane fuel is recommended? etc.

Ask them to write down the answers and when the test is over let each person mark his own paper. Call out the answers, then afterwards ask anyone who has them all correct to raise his hand, then one wrong, two wrong and so on, until you have accounted for the score of the whole group.

Being able to explain policies, procedures, and systems to your staff and your colleagues will not only help the training programme; it helps improve communication within your company, assists in building a company-wide team spirit, and reinforces your position as the team leader. It is a skill which is well worth practising!

Questions

1. Name the three stages involved in the lecture.
2. What additional two stages are used in the group instruction technique and why are they used?

7. Understanding complaints and grievances

A complaint is not the same thing as a grievance. A complaint occurs when somebody tells you about his dissatisfaction or problem, but the grievance is the dissatisfaction itself. The complaint is the effect and the grievance is the cause. Many people have grievances which they never express in words but they have other ways of expressing them. Sometimes people's work will deteriorate in quantity or quality, they may become moody or depressed, or cause dissatisfaction among those around them. The usual cheerful talkative employee may become quiet, or the unobtrusive employee may start banging about. Preoccupation may cause inattention or carelessness so that an accident occurs, or an employee may leave the job altogether to try and escape the cause of the trouble. This cause-and-effect relationship is shown in Fig. 7.1.

If there is no complaint the supervisor may not realize that there is a problem at all and simply attribute these effects to today's attitudes. But a complaint gives the supervisor something to go on, something to account for the drop in productivity and to show that action needs to be taken to put it right. When people feel free to complain to you, their complaints will not be aggravated through being repressed. You may receive more of them, but they are less likely to be serious ones.

Grievances in disguise

Though complaints show that something is wrong, they do not always tell you accurately what the problem is.

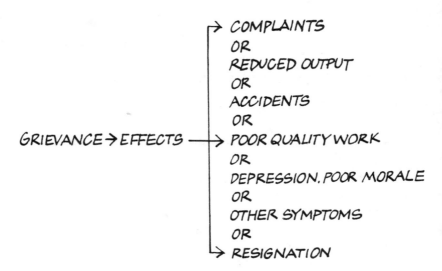

GRIEVANCE → EFFECTS ⟶
- → COMPLAINTS
- OR
- REDUCED OUTPUT
- OR
- ACCIDENTS
- OR
- POOR QUALITY WORK
- OR
- DEPRESSION, POOR MORALE
- OR
- OTHER SYMPTOMS
- OR
- → RESIGNATION

Figure 7.1 Effect of grievances

A person may let off steam by complaining about the tools provided, when the real problem is the fact that the supervisor is suspected of favouritism. Home problems can cause trouble at work so that a normally cooperative and steady employee flies off the handle for no apparent reason until you find that he or she hasn't slept for three nights as a result of the baby's night-time feeding troubles; and most people would expect their spouse to be especially outspoken about slipping on a roller skate in the front garden after having a bad day at the office. Avoid being inquisitive about an employee's personal affairs but don't go to the other extreme. Some supervisors take the attitude: 'I'm not concerned with people's personal problems. They can leave them at the gate when they clock on and pick them up again when they go home.' It would be very convenient if we could all switch our troubles off and on like that, but of course we can't.

There are many things that make people disguise their troubles. Sometimes they do so because their real grievance puts them in an unfavourable light or makes them look absurd

DIAGNOSE THE GRIEVANCE

or they may be afraid to admit it even to themselves, or the true problem may be so complex that it defies definition. This means that the supervisor has to diagnose the grievance and see what lies behind the apparent problem. This diagnosis is not so difficult if you remember that our grievances exist in the gap or deficit between what we want and what we are getting. When we believe that we are being denied those things we have a right to, a grievance results. We may be denied the things we need in our workplace—such as a reasonable wage, satisfactory work, security, adequate equipment, companionship, good working conditions and a reasonable boss. On the other hand, our grievances may have nothing to do with work at all. We need health, a happy and tranquil home life, three square meals a day, hobbies and time to enjoy them, a pleasant home and a chance to give the children at least as good a start in life as we had. If any of these hopes are not fulfilled a feeling of deprivation may cause a grievance.

To identify the root cause of an employee's problem you should examine in what way life is dealing out less than he or she expects, because that gap between hopes and reality is the breeding ground of grievances. If you could abolish the deficit you would eliminate the grievance. The problem is that, as stated in chapter 1, not everybody has the same needs. In some measure we all want certain things, but not with the same intensity. The young person usually looks for more money before security of employment, the extrovert wants company, while another will sacrifice anything else for the satisfaction of having an enjoyable job. It all boils down to knowing your staff.

Be interested in what they want and, as far as you can, help them to achieve it through their work. Commonsense warns against giving people advice and judgement on personal or private matters, but if an employee seeks your guidance you can either help him or her to think matters out, or you can put the person in contact with the appropriate organization—for example, the Citizen's Advice Bureau, or personnel department, if you have one.

Five rules for grievance interviews

It is not always possible to know all the staff working under you. We are moved around and so are those whom we supervise, and the sheer number of people some of us have to control may make it difficult to know more than their names. This is where the five rules come in. They are a guide to anyone who has to interview a person with a grievance and they provide the best way of getting to the root of the problem.

Rule 1—Listen and do not interrupt

The employee is probably tense and all wound up with the complaint so wait for the storm to subside. Don't correct points of detail even if they are inaccurate—allow the whole case to be presented. You may later have to correct certain inaccuracies but wait until the end. By letting the employee talk you have not conceded anything which you may later regret.

Rule 2—Show interest

Have you ever told your grievance to somebody who fiddled about in the filing cabinet, yawned, made an irrelevant telephone call, and kept looking at the clock? The individual's grievance may be the most important thing in the world to him or her so try to look at it as if it were your own and show real interest.

Rule 3—Do not get drawn into an argument

This is easier said than done but if you follow Rule 1 an argument is less likely to develop. If you should come to a stalemate amounting to a 'yes I did—no you didn't' deadlock, try another tack.

Rule 4—Repeat back in your own words what has been said

By stating the problem in your own words you ensure that you have understood the story correctly and you prove you have listened. This leaves no doubt as to your attentiveness, and helps the employee to agree with at least something you are saying and to consider the problem objectively. Many people who are unwilling to come straight out with their real grievances try out the supervisor's receptiveness with a side issue first. If that is sympathetically received they bring out the real problem.

Rule 5—Beware of promises

An obvious one this. Do not make any promises unless you know you can deliver.

Not only do these five rules enable you to come to grips with the real hidden problem if there is one, but they also have a useful side-effect. You will find that even if, despite all your efforts at finding a solution to the person's problem, it is impossible to solve it, you will nevertheless have lessened the grievance. There is something in the process of sharing a problem with another person, defining it, appreciating it and trying to do something about it, which alleviates the stress.

To summarize:

1. Don't repress complaints.
2. Don't always take them at their face value. There may be something behind them.
3. You will understand grievances better if you understand your staff, what each wants out of life, and where their hopes are not being realized.
4. Use the five rules for dealing with complaints.

Know your company's grievance procedure

In most companies there is a right and wrong way for staff to raise any complaints they have. Find out, if you do not already know, what the right way is. Your personnel officer or, if you haven't one, your general manager or works manager will be able to tell you. The usual channel is as follows (we will assume that there is a union representative, but of course the procedure is shorter if there is not):

1. The employee with a complaint first talks to the supervisor.
2. If dissatisfied with the result, the employee takes it to the union representative who in turn takes it up again with the supervisor.
3. If no settlement results the union representative takes it up with higher management.

It is important to insist on the fact that an employee should approach you in person as the supervisor in the first instance and not ask the representative to do so. You should also try to persuade the latter to see the wisdom of this. Most problems do not warrant union intervention; the representative is there in reserve for those that do. The exception to this rule is when the problem is one that affects everybody, such as car parks or canteens, and then naturally the shop steward will take it up as the legitimate spokesman for the staff as a whole.

If individual complaints were constantly short-circuiting you and going straight to the union representative, it could be that you were not very approachable and in that case you would need to polish up on the five rules!

Table 7.1 Checklist on handling complaints and grievances

Questions	×✓	Notes
1. Do you make time at the earliest opportunity to listen when there is the slightest hint of a grievance?		
2. Do you find a suitable time and place?		
3. Do you avoid having a desk or table between you and the person who is complaining?		
4. Do you show real undivided interest?		
5. If the union representative raises an individual's problem which is new to you, do you tactfully point out that the employee should have come to you about it first?		
6. Do you avoid a sterile argument?		
7. Do you summarize the complaint(s) in order to check the accuracy of your interpretation?		
8. Are you careful not to give a promise when you are not sure you can fulfil it?		

Questions

1. As a supervisor you find that the union representative is taking employees' grievances to your department head and by-passing you. What steps can you take to prevent this happening?
2. What rules do you think apply to grievance interviewing?
3. What kind of emotional problems do employees sometimes have to face at work?
4. Two employees are frightened of losing their jobs, and this insecurity is affecting their work. How would you deal with this situation?

8. *Introducing changes*

Changes are occurring so fast nowadays that your company is probably employing techniques, tools and machinery that were not even invented five years ago, and it is certain that the next five years will bring even greater innovations. Machines and systems respond quickly to changes and do not groan very much at the introduction of them, but people are different. One eminent doctor and philosopher says that it is the failure of our organism to respond to modern life in appropriate ways which produces so much mental ill-health and so much physical sickness with psychological origins. We cannot easily adapt to new circumstances and new ways of doing things. Our reaction when faced with them is often one of fear and obstructiveness.

Why should this be so? One of the main reasons for resistance to new ideas is the fact that they appear to be a criticism of the old way of doing things. The need to innovate is taken to mean that something was wrong with the old way and by implication with those who were using it. Then there is the fear of the unknown. 'What are these changes going to be, and what effect will they have on me?' People want to know, for many are afraid of being unable to cope with a new set-up, and of being criticized for doing the job wrongly. 'Will I look a fool for not catching on quickly? Will some of these youngsters be doing the job better than I can?' The old rut is comfortable and it hurts to move out of it, especially if you are no longer young and think that you might be on the scrap heap before long under the new scheme of things.

There is also the fact that changes often break up people's groupings, separating friends and putting them with people they know less well—perhaps even isolating them altogether.

WILL I LOOK A FOOL?

Example

A shoemaking firm changed over one of its factories from batch production to flow-line production some years ago. Under the old batch-production system the operators used to sit facing each other round a table, an arrangement which permitted them to exchange views and jokes together. The flow-line arrangement made this impossible because an operator could only see the backs of the people in front and one person on each side by a turn of the head. People felt badly about it at first and several years later at teabreaks when staff were free to have a talk they tended to seek out those same people with whom they formerly worked on batch-production. It shows how much people like to stay together, and resist the break-up of their groups.

There may be a loss of earnings as a result of the new way of doing the job or perhaps the money may be better but one's skill becomes redundant. Many shorthand-typists will not accept work as copy typists because they do not want to lose their shorthand. Again, although someone may be no worse off financially, others who were inferior in status or skill have now caught up because of the new technologies which have done away with the advantages that skills used to confer. This means they are no longer the top wage earners—a bitter pill for some to swallow. Sometimes, although one is prepared to forget all these objections to change and give it a try, a trade union sees real danger and imposes its veto so that solidarity with fellow workers forbids acceptance. Resistance to change has always been there, hidden, of course, but whereas in the old days people had to tolerate it in silence, now they can and do express themselves more freely.

How can you get people to accept change?

It is in everybody's interest— management, the staff, and the public who buy the products—that new and better ways should be found and put into effect. You have a vital part to play in winning the staff's acceptance for new ideas. You are expected to implement top management's policy, and if this includes the adoption of new working methods you must assist in that process.

It is of no use telling people to 'like it or lump it', and neither is it a responsible sort of attitude to say 'It has got to be done in this new way because the boss says so.' People must be given the reasons for the changes that are being made, and the supervisor has to play the necessary part in putting them across even if not personally in agreement with them. This may sound hard and it may go against the grain to have to advocate something you do not really want, but that is your duty. Privately, out of the staff's hearing, you should put your case to your own superior, giving the reasons why you think the proposed innovation is wrong; if your opinion is over-ruled then you must accept the decision. The only alternative to this way of running a business would be to have 'committee management' and this would be far too slow in today's competitive world. The manager must manage. Those are the rules of the game, so don't be lukewarm about new methods and procedures. Unless you give them your support, you cannot expect the staff to go along with them. Besides not being lukewarm, what else can you do to get people to accept changes? And what can top management do?

Tell people well in advance

It is the unexpected which shocks us most. When we know that something is going to happen in six months' time, we accustom ourselves to the thought and make our own private preparations. News of a transfer may mean all sorts of arrangements concerning the house, the children's school, hire purchase and so on. So tell people well in advance of things that will affect them.

Chip away at the reasons for resisting the new proposals

Suppose we consider any situation as temporary; an equilibrium between the forces for change and the forces for keeping things as they are, as shown in Fig. 8.1

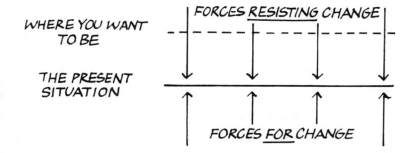

Figure 8.1 Temporary equilibrium

If you want to introduce a change and simply increase the 'upward' pressure in order to get there, you may well find that the opposition redoubles its resistance in order to maintain things as they are. A more effective approach would be to remove the *reasons* for resistance by chipping away at them from behind.

Example

Most young householders may at some time or other be in this situation. There are reasons why they would like to move, and reasons against. Let us suppose the wife is keen on moving but the husband is less enthusiastic. The forces for change are that the house is too small and not suitable for entertaining their new circle of friends.

The forces against are: the upheaval, removal costs, a bigger mortgage, and the redecorating which would have to be done in the new house.

The more she presses for the move (frontal assault) the more resistance she may meet ('when George digs his heels in . . .'). But if she carefully identifies his real reasons for resistance and satisfactorily deals with each objection, George may soon find he is all for it!

Introducing changes **93**

Modesty pays

Because innovation is often viewed as a criticism of the old ways of doing things, commonsense dictates modesty in bringing in new ideas. 'I told you so' will make people's hackles rise and they will secretly hope to see you fall flat on your face.

Don't make exaggerated claims in advance

Some supervisors are so keen to see a different method introduced that they oversell it, and when it does not achieve all that is expected of it, people regard it as a failure. So don't get carried away with your own enthusiasm and lead people to expect too much.

Don't be shaken by criticism and ridicule. Have determination and a broad back

---

Example

The management of the Gresham Press at Old Woking had a mural painted on one of their walls as part of a plan to make the working environment more pleasant. There were some humorous remarks about it at first but here is what one of the firm's supervisors had to say: 'They may make fun of the new picture on the wall, but they are secretly proud of it.' Managing, whether you are a supervisor or a general manager, can be a lonely job, and you have to stick to your guns when you know you are in the right.

Try to introduce changes gradually

Some changes can only be made drastically. But people will accept *gradual* change more readily, innovations which are made little by little so that as one success is scored it provides a basis for acceptance of the next round. Consider whether this can be done in your case. It often gives people time to adapt to the new trends if they are embarked upon in a gradual way.

You can make the change in one section, or for a trial period to start with.

Allow people to have their say and report back to management the comments you hear

Management needs to know what the employees say, and they like to know that their comments are being listened to and their feelings considered. When the supervisor won't listen and says with an air of finality: 'That's company policy', it can be very frustrating. It is this sort of thing that makes staff go to their union representative who then goes straight to the top, by-passing the immediate superior. It is true that some managements encourage this by not keeping the supervisor as well informed as they ought, but don't expect to be spoonfed with information all the time. If you don't know, ask.

Involve people in the change

Use your team's experience and ingenuity by explaining the proposal and asking for their opinion. Then they will not be so likely to regard it as something alien, threatening their security and labelling them as 'out of date'. They will consider the change as partly their own, and take a proprietary interest in making it work.

Example

A Japanese group bought out a ball bearing company who could make only a slender profit in this highly competitive market. With it came many of the experienced engineers who had helped to establish it as a world leader. The miniature bearings were first ground to an approximate size and then honed to exactly the right tolerances. When the Japanese production people took over they told the British and American engineers: 'Cycle time too long for grinding. You must speed up the process.' This the engineers reluctantly did but one confessed privately that he felt justified in his opposition when the time saved on the grinding was doubly lost on the honing. 'We had been right all along,' he said, 'they should have listened to us. In the end they had to go back to our way.'

Next time somebody stands by and lets you flounder instead of giving you a tip which would have averted the mistake, ask yourself whether you could have sought more help rather than trying to go it alone. And, of course, when the outcome is successful you have to see that all who helped get the credit.

Maintain the change

All changes have unforeseen side-effects, so it is important to appraise and maintain the new method. Do not forget to make the necessary adjustments either to the system itself, or to the surrounding circumstances.

What's in it for the staff?

Change is uncomfortable but usually profitable. It is perhaps unreasonable to expect those affected to have all the discomfort and none of the profit. In some cases the benefit is not a direct financial one. It may take the form of greater security because by virtue of the change the company becomes more competitive and better able to retain its share of the trade. In other instances an immediate increase in productivity and profitability may result. If management waits for the union to fight for a share and then gradually yields, it will have to pay anyway, but in addition to the money it will pay in lost cooperation and goodwill. It is surely far better to say 'This is our saving. What share can we give our employees?'

In the short run changes do sometimes affect people adversely and these harmful results must be guarded against, but change should mean a better life for everybody. Your responsibility as a supervisor is to help it along and try to make it painless.

Table 8.1 Checklist on introducing changes

Questions	×✓	Notes
1. Do you explain the reasons for changes?		
2. Do you explain what benefits will be derived from this particular change?		
3. Do you tell everybody who will be affected?		
4. Do you tell them soon enough?		
5. Do you give them a chance to comment?		
6. Do you listen to their suggestions?		
7. If you have to reject a suggestion do you tell them why?		
8. Do you pass on to your superior any significant comments?		
9. Do you consider whether this particular change would be better introduced gradually?		
10. Do you consider how it will affect the employee's self-respect? security? sense of belonging to a team?		
11. Can you provide a way in which people can save face in accepting the change?		
12. Do you consider what support and assistance you can give to people to help them during this change?		
13. Are you patient and tolerant with those who will now find the going harder?		
14. Are you firm in your ultimate objectives?		
15. Are you prepared to make adjustments in your plans for getting there?		
16. Do you carefully consider the real objections to a particular change and chip away at them from behind?		

Questions

1. Unrest is often caused by changes. If you were the general manager, outline the steps you would take to introduce a major change in the company's operations.
2. Of what importance is effective communication when changes are being introduced at work?
3. What are the biggest obstacles to change? (Concentrate on the human element.)
4. What skills does a supervisor need in order to win acceptance of change?

9. Reducing disciplinary problems

When people work in a company where the wages are good and the atmosphere friendly, where they have a pride in the end product and their part in producing it, where they know where they stand with management and are adequately informed—under these conditions you do not often find that people break regulations. The first essential for good order is to provide good leadership by following the guidelines which are given in Chapter 1 and 2. Most people want to be able to carry on with their work in peace and are sensible enough to see that without rules and procedures to follow, without respect for supervisors, there would be anarchy. They themselves toe the line and you owe it not only to yourself but to the law-abiders as well to see that the minority, too, behave in a responsible way.

Whether you find this easy or difficult depends partly on circumstances. Firstly, the temptation to break regulations in the company should, as far as possible, be removed. For example, in oil refineries the temptation to smoke in areas where it is forbidden is diminished by setting aside a special smoking area in which people are free to light up. Don't just accept a situation in which people are tempted to break a rule.

Top management may not be aware of how unreasonable the rule is, so put up your recommendation on how it could be changed, giving your reasons. You may have to make the regulations impossible to break. If you are a parent you know that you not only have to tell young Gary not to move the TV set to his bedroom . . . you fix it to the floor as well.

Secondly, it is more difficult for supervisors to keep people in line when higher management takes away their authority by not keeping them informed of things they should know, by not supporting them in actions they take, frequently reversing their decisions, or by giving orders directly to those under their control without reference to the supervisor in charge. If this happens to you, point out tactfully to your chief that it will make his job easier in the long run if he helps you by supporting you, informing you and applying managerial control through you, instead of bypassing your position and undermining your authority.

What the manager or supervisor can do to reduce disciplinary problems

Set a good example The way you do your job, how tidily you work, what time you arrive in the morning, the attitude you show towards management—these things will speak much louder and will constantly affect the attitudes of those under your control. If you privately think that some company regulations are unwise, or that a policy is wrong, tell your superior, but don't broadcast your disagreement to the staff. That will undermine their confidence in you and management.

Be friendly but not familiar Familiarity is overstepping the mark with nicknames, practical jokes and personal remarks. You have to be friendly, approachable and talk to all of your people as equals.

Build a friendly atmosphere—a family feeling A sense of common purpose goes a long way in establishing a family spirit, so keep on reminding people of the common goals and everybody's part in achieving them.

When recruiting, try to select people who are going to fit in well with your existing team. As the work pressure builds up, a good relationship between the staff will help them all to tackle the challenge calmly and with good humour.

Try to avoid situations in which an employee has two bosses   When an employee is responsible to two people, such as yourself and a colleague of yours, difficulties can arise. If you find yourself sharing a subordinate, extreme tact is needed. Avoid this situation if you can.

Earn their respect   Respect each one of *them*, and you are 90 per cent of the way there.

Make sure the rules are known   Learn and keep to the rules yourself, and ensure that nobody can plead ignorance if they break the rules. Besides ensuring that you give people a fair deal, knowing the rule-book will boost your self-confidence.

Recognize individuals' qualities   No two people will have the same strengths and weaknesses. It is your job to bring out the strengths that are there, compensating for the weaknesses. Ensure that everybody in the group is known for some particular quality.

Keep everybody in the picture   Unless they all know where they are going and how they are doing, dissensions will arise, and your leadership may be challenged by somebody in the group who *does* communicate.

Do not allow poor performers to stay beyond their probationary period   If your company has a probationary period for new employees and you have your doubts about whether a particular person will make the grade, or whether their attitude and behaviour will upset the harmony with your team, think carefully before confirming the appointment. When a person has been employed for 2 years and is dismissed after that period of time, he or she may take the employer to an Industrial Tribunal for unfair dismissal. So if you have your doubts about a particular employee, weigh up the situation well before the end of the 2 years. (For anyone employed before 1 June 1985 the period is one year, not two, in companies employing more than 20 people.)

Put square pegs in square holes, and make sure that the section heads you appoint are good leaders Any employee who is in the wrong job will not be entirely happy and may cause problems. This is particularly so with a team leader who may be good on the technical side but hopeless as a supervisor. Training may help to adapt the person who is a misfit, but there is no real substitute for careful selection at all levels.

Don't have favourites Before you were a manager you could choose your friends and keep away from those you didn't want to bother with, but now you have to be available to all employees.

Expect high standards Research has shown that the best results are obtained by managers who expect the highest standards, demonstrating confidence in people's ability and inclination to do a job well and to observe the rules in doing so. Leniency and tolerance of slack standards soon lead to discontent and the

DON'T HAVE FAVOURITES

breakdown of discipline. Let everybody know that you expect the best they are capable of.

Give forewarnings Occasionally regulations which have been allowed to lapse have to be re-established suddenly. When this occurs give a forewarning and the reasons for tightening up. Legally you may be safe in taking action without doing so, but the employee affected will justifiably ask 'Why pick on me?'

Find out what authority you have If you have the responsibility for maintaining good order in your department you must have a certain amount of authority although you probably have to check with others before using some of it. It will make your job easier if you can find out exactly what powers have been granted to you. Try filling in the following analysis by putting a tick in the appropriate column. If in doubt, ask your superior to give a ruling. Add in any other actions or responsibilities on which your authority is not clear.

Table 9.1 Checklist of areas of authority

Action	Complete authority	Obtain approval first	Recommend only
Manpower Increase manpower pay roll Recruit replacements Report on probationary employees Transfer employees within your department Arrange transfer with other departments Lay people off for lack of work			

Table 9.1 (*continued*)

Action	Complete authority	Obtain approval first	Recommend only
Discipline Give written reprimand Suspend from work Discharge (very rare)			
Grievances Listen to grievances in the first instance Accept written grievances from trade unions Give written replies to these			
Time off Grant leave of absence Allow people to go home early in special circumstances			
Training and education Carry out on-the-job training Prepare apprentice-training rosters Send people on courses Arrange grants for company-sponsored studies			
Safety Stop people working when there is a risk			

Action	Complete authority	Obtain approval first	Recommend only
Take unsafe tools and machinery out of service Send employees for first aid Make out accident reports			
Services Requisition internal transport, lifting tackle, etc. Call on maintenance services Call on electrical services			
Quality Reject products Be final judge on whether a product will pass			

Reprimands

The foregoing points dealt with keeping good order and preventing acts of indiscipline. If a reprimand *must* be given, how do you go about this? Here are some tips which will help you next time you have to reprimand. (Remember that your purpose is to prevent a recurrence and not to punish the person. If you can achieve this without applying sanctions so much the better.)

Don't turn a blind eye

If somebody comes in late, goes off early, works a machine without a guard or does anything else against the rules, don't turn a blind eye. By doing so, you are implying that it doesn't matter. Let the employee see that you have noticed and that you don't expect it to happen again. It is better to do this at the time, provided that by doing so you do not make the person look small in front of others.

Don't act in anger

A spontaneous and justified outburst does sometimes get results but it is usually dangerous to give way to this impulse. So often all the facts are not available and one is left looking a fool because the employee was in the right. Cool down, count to ten, say you want to see the person later—anything to give you time to deal calmly with the situation.

Prepare for the interview

Get the facts. If the problem is poor quality work, obtain the scrap figures or any error frequency records so that you can put the facts on the table. You will at least then both be starting on common ground with the same factual evidence to go on. Make time for the interview and hold it in private. If it is going to be a long session make sure the venue is also comfortable and quiet.

Plan your approach. What sort of person are you dealing with, on what wavelength? Will you start with a problem which you know is uppermost in his or her mind? If you haven't spoken to him or her for a long time perhaps you may have to re-establish contact first. One foreman in a machine shop wanted to caution an overhead crane operator for bad time-keeping, but had not communicated with the operator except by hand signals for seven years. Obviously there was some preparatory work to be done there. In most cases the sandwich method works well—that is, a kick in the pants in between two pats on the back.

The two-stage interview

It is usually better to conduct the interview in two parts.

1. *Let the employee explain* Outline the problem as you see it. Do not do this aggressively, and do not judge too quickly or

react too strongly at this stage. Take time to think. Draw out all the facts and feelings, including whether the person is upset by a particular event. At this stage your prime purpose is to ensure that you fully understand the situation.

When you have done this you will probably want to verify the accuracy or talk it over with your boss. Then you can weigh and decide. Consider the range of alternatives at this point. Perhaps the employee needs training, a change of job, time to assess the situation, or a warning. Select the best alternative, but foresee the snags in pursuing it. For example, if dismissal is the only answer, how is your depleted team going to meet that important deadline?

Take the employee's record into account. It is not favouritism simply to caution someone who, for the first time in a year, works the machine without a guard—nor is it victimization to suspend someone who does the same thing but who has a long history of unsafe practices and has been involved in one or two accidents.

After you have gathered all the facts, *develop a range of possible courses of action*. The chapter entitled 'Using initiative when work is delegated to you' provides a number of questions which you can ask yourself in order to produce a variety of possible remedies. The more options you can develop the better will be your chance of producing the ideal answer. Cross off the non-starters and tick your best choice; sometimes you may wish to combine courses of action (e.g., transfer and retrain).

2. *Advise him of your decision* If your company is unionized your disciplinary procedure will probably require the presence of the union representative at this stage.

Follow up

After you have taken your action, monitor the employee's performance. How well is the person learning the new job? If the problem was lateness, absenteeism, or poor performance, has there been an improvement? Let the person know *when* you

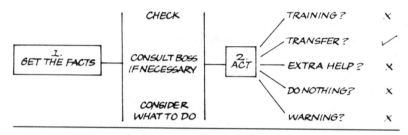

EXAMPLE

A WORKER REFUSED TO OPERATE A BLOCK AND TACKLE OVER A CHEMICAL VAT. THE SUPERVISOR EVENTUALLY FOUND OUT THAT THE FUMES WERE CAUSING RESPIRATORY TROUBLES WHICH THE EMPLOYEE WAS RELUCTANT TO ADMIT, AND THE REMEDY WAS A CHANGE OF JOB

1. GET THE FACTS — CHECK — CONSULT BOSS IF NECESSARY — CONSIDER WHAT TO DO

2. ACT — TRAINING? X — TRANSFER? ✓ — EXTRA HELP? X — DO NOTHING? X — WARNING? X

Figure 9.1 The two-stage interview

are going to review progress, and be sure you discuss it together on that day. Has the problem been solved? What further action is needed?

Written notes

If you have to leave a note in writing to convey what seems to you a very mild rebuke, think again. It is always better to communicate this kind of message face to face. The written word is so often misinterpreted unless explained and discussed.

Don't reprimand in front of others

If you do you will belittle and arouse resentment.

Be careful when using wit

The humorous remark or witty observation is fine when there is a strong enough mutual understanding for it to be taken lightheartedly. The trouble is that witty criticisms can be taken as sarcasm and that invites rejoinders.

Use the 'law of the situation'

If you want to correct people you must appeal to their reason by telling them why they are expected to do whatever it is you are asking them to do. Instead of saying 'I'm telling you to do this'

DON'T REPRIMAND HIM IN FRONT OF OTHERS

you say 'This is the situation, therefore this is what has to be done.' It is the situation which has laid down the law, not the supervisor. The appeal to a person's reason enables you to secure cooperation and this applies whether you are talking to your subordinate, colleague or even your boss.

Let the union know

Company policy varies on this point but many supervisors find it pays to tell the union representative what has happened (assuming you find out first!) and what you propose to do. Some supervisors like to have the shop steward in attendance during the informal hearing of what the person has to say about the infraction. In most cases it seems good sense to keep the employee's representative in the picture, because it ensures that both union and management are working on the same set of facts and there is no distortion of the truth about what happened and what was said.

Consider suspension without pay

There are two situations in which this can be used. The first is an interim measure with the object of removing from the workplace an employee who, through a presumed fault, such as being intoxicated or involved in a brawl, is temporarily not in a fit state to work. In this case the employee should be required to go home for the rest of the shift and report next day when appropriate action would be taken.

The other situation is when it is decided to impose suspension as a penalty. This measure should only be used if the employee's contract of employment provides for it, or if it is accepted by custom and practice. It should only be taken with the approval of the person in your organization who is responsible for industrial relations. The trade union will sometimes accept it as a preferable alternative to dismissal.

Know and use the company's disciplinary procedure

Most companies have drawn up a disciplinary procedure, and if there is a union it will almost certainly have been agreed. It is important that you should find out if such a procedure exists in your own organization and that you should know and observe it, because failure to do so would undermine your position. Procedures of this kind normally operate as follows:

1. The first step is a verbal warning or, in the case of more serious misconduct, a written warning setting out the circumstances.

2. No employee should be dismissed for a first breach of discipline except in the case of gross misconduct.

3. Action on any further misconduct, for example, final warning, suspension or dismissal, should be recorded in writing.

4. Details of disciplinary action should be given in writing to the employee and to the union representative if the employee so wishes.

5. No disciplinary action should be taken against a shop steward until the circumstances of the case have been discussed with a full-time official of the union concerned.

Good discipline is a matter of adjustment Obviously the best discipline is to be found in a department where reprimands are unnecessary, and your aim must always be to achieve that state of affairs.

Table 9.2 Checklist on good order

Questions	×✓	*Notes*
1. Are company regulations observed in your department?		
2. Do employees avoid wasting their time or others' time?		
3. Are instructions promptly and willingly carried out?		
4. Do they do a good day's work, even in your absence?		
5. Do they set a good example to other departments, e.g., not stopping their work to chatter, etc.?		
6. Do you know all your team individually?		
7. Are you fair in your treatment of staff?		
8. Do you treat them with due consideration of their self-respect?		
9. Do you get people to use self-discipline?		
10. Is there any pilfering?		
11. Do staff take undue advantage of normal breaks?		
12. Are there cleanliness and good housekeeping?		
13. Do you set a good example?		
14. Do you know the extent and limits of your authority in suspending or dismissing?		

Table 9.2 (*continued*)

Questions	×✓	Notes
15. Do you avoid undermining your subordinates?		
16. Do your subordinates respect your position and not bypass you to the boss?		
17. Do you avoid implying 'It's the boss's order, not mine?'		
18. Do you give instructions clearly and confidently?		
19. Do your people observe the safety regulations?		
20. Is there a low accident rate?		
21. Is there a good industrial relationship with the union representatives?		
22. Do you know the company's disciplinary procedures?		
23. Do you know employer–employee law as it affects you?		

Questions

1. How would you reprimand an employee for careless, poor quality work?
2. How can the supervisor obtain good discipline in his team?
3. One of your staff is continually going to your manager with small complaints even though you have asked them to come to you first. How can you deal with this situation?
4. An employee often leaves the workplace and spends long periods in the cloakroom. What would you do about this?
5. How is discipline affected when a person has more than one boss?
6. A skilled operator who does excellent work and has never had an accident regularly arrives at the car park at 7.30 a.m. and, it is said, sits in the car drinking until 8.00 a.m. By 8.00 a.m., when work starts, the smell of alcohol is obvious. What should you do about this?

10. *Your responsibility for communication*

Dinosaur Ltd

The Sauropoda Dinosaur had communication problems. It was possible for a mesozoic midge to raise lumps on his tail that had practically gone septic by the time the news reached the

`DINO-SORE`

brain. So another brain was installed halfway along. Its job was to help out with communication by relaying messages and generally looking after the flow of information to and from the limbs under its control.

Communication is an important part of the supervisor's job in industry. In the very early stages of the development of a business the owner can deal directly with the staff, telling them about its competitive position and the effects of demand and markets upon it. In return, the owner should be interested in them as individuals, knowing and making allowances for them and their problems, limitations and special aptitudes.

Later would come the dinosaur stage—the business would grow, the owner become removed from the staff owing to other management and business preoccupations, and a supervisor would be necessary in each department. Eventually two or three more levels of management would come between the owner and the supervisor and by then it would be important to do something to maintain communication.

The founder would still try to circulate as often as possible but would be forced to delegate the personal contact and exchange of opinions, feelings and information to the supervisor.

Some supervisors look at the elaborate communication network in their companies. They see:

the company magazine
the bulletin
the noticeboard
the loudspeaker system

and they wash their hands of all responsibility for passing and receiving information: 'I don't need to bother now—top management is communicating direct.' They forget that you cannot *discuss* with a magazine, bulletin or noticeboard and that you can read the wrong message between the lines. All these are only aids to communication. They are better than no communication at all but they are not personal enough, there is no opportunity for question and answer, and you cannot see the expression on the other person's face.

The supervisor should be the direct personal link between the staff and top management. You have a clear responsibility to communicate downwards to staff and upwards to your manager.

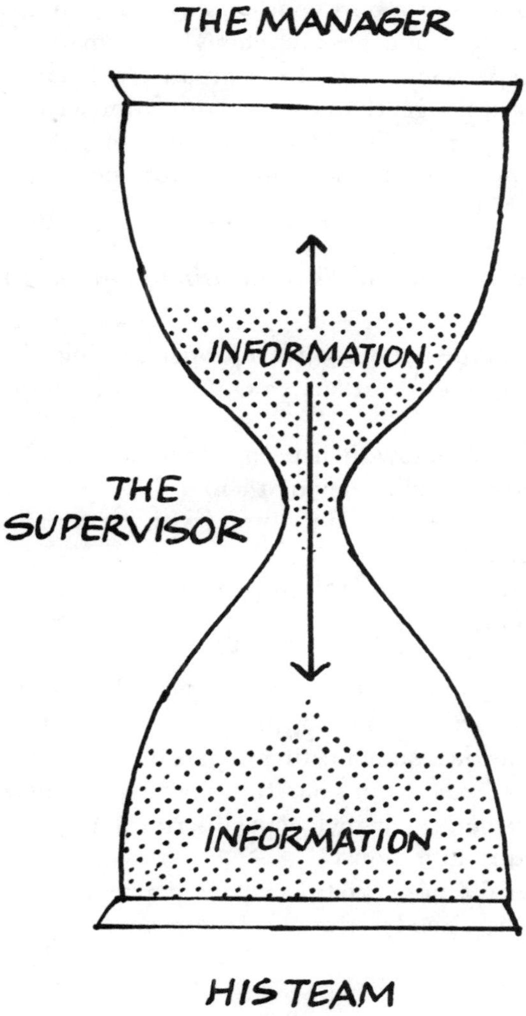

Figure 10.1 Lines of communication

Communicating downwards

You must interpret management's policy decisions and actions favourably to your staff. If you disagree with them you may say so to management, but your disagreement is not for publication and you are bound to support your employer in public.

You should obtain and pass on enough information about the job, the department and the company, to enable your people to work intelligently and with the enthusiasm which comes of knowing what it is all for. If senior management does not volunteer much information, don't wait to be told, ask.

There are five main methods of keeping your staff in the picture

1. Make sure that new staff receive a proper briefing when you induct them into the department (see the chapter on Induction).
2. Ensure that they know their terms of reference and targets and their progress in achieving them.
3. Make a point of having daily contact with every member of your staff in order to:
   - set standards (tidiness, safety, personal appearance, punctuality, conduct, etc.);
   - show appreciation;
   - give constructive criticism or guidance where needed;
   - ask if there are questions or problems and sort them out.
4. Call the occasional staff meeting to pass on information you may have received from your superior, explain plans and impending changes, or review past performance as a basis for your future intentions.
5. Ensure that the noticeboard in your department is up to date, tidy, and a good testimony of the importance you place on communication.

Example

The National Trust maintains hundreds of estates, stately homes, forests, and long stretches of coastline in the UK, employing about 2000 permanent staff and a large number of short-term employees under such schemes as the YTS and Community Projects. Some of their supervisors complain that quite a few of the youngsters have very little interest in their work and are difficult to motivate, but not so a supervisor I met in Cornwall, whom I shall refer to as Tom. At the beginning of each day, he and his team of twelve teenage boys and girls gathered together for a 'crib' (Cornish for tea break) lasting 15 minutes. They would review the day's work, dividing up the tasks. Two particularly liked making fires with the dead branches or heather which had been cut the previous day. He called those his 'pyromaniacs'. Others liked using the chain saw, others liked repairing fencing, and then there were the chores which required everyone to lend a hand, such as clearing the acres of wild blackthorn bushes.

Tom knew he could not watch all of them all of the time, since they would be scattered over 10 square miles or more. But his 15-minute crib break was his opportunity to motivate them for the day, congratulating them on yesterday's achievements, commenting on any substandard work, setting goals for the new day, and letting everyone know that he or she was a vital member of a team doing an important job. If it was anybody's birthday, Tom knew and remembered. Driving test results, sporting activities, social events would all be discussed at crib time. Tom's team didn't just see themselves as being kept off the streets—they were maintaining the amenities of Cornwall as a tourist attraction, and preparing themselves for a meaningful working life.

No doubt some will become supervisors and take a leaf out of Tom's book when it comes to communication, explaining why the job is important, praising, setting standards, and being prepared to listen to the views and feelings of the team.

Communicating upwards

Your chief is interested in two main items, the *staff* and the *work*.

The staff

It is true that joint consultative committees have an important part to play in keeping top management in touch with the staff's opinions and ideas, but so have all supervisors.

1. You should keep your chief informed about people's problems, feelings, reactions and ideas.
2. Besides being management's advocate to the employees you should be their advocate to management. In companies where section leaders leave all this to the union, the shop stewards and full-time officials spend too much of their time making up for management's own poor communication. It is understandable if from there they go on to start trying to run the business.

The work

You should keep your boss in the picture about what is happening in your area so that he or she is not caught unawares. For example it would look pretty incompetent if in the dining room another department head commented: 'I see you had a nasty accident in "B" Machine Shop this morning', and your boss knew nothing about it. Here are the main classifications of information needed from you:

● *Progress on long-term work* Brief your manager as often as required about how any major project is developing. Perhaps the project involves the planned standardization of equipment by means of specified replacements to worn-out non-standard machinery, or it may be the long-term training of your staff to make the section more flexible. Give the boss an up-to-date mental picture of how such jobs are going along.

● *Exceptional events* You can overdo progress reporting. It would be time-wasting for everybody to report frequently that everything is OK, so we use the 'management by exception'

YOU CAN OFTEN FORESEE PROBLEMS
MORE EASILY THAN THE BOSS

principle, which means that you only report when there is something significant to say. The next four classifications are examples of significant events which would warrant reporting upwards.

● *Completion of assignment*   Suppose the filing system has had to be reorganized and old documents separated off into the dead file store. Your superior will expect to be told when you have done the job.

● *Deviation from plan*   The job is scheduled for completion on 1 May, but you are behind because two of the staff have been away sick and one of your suppliers was late with a delivery. It is important to let the boss know this so that steps can be taken to speed the job up further along the line, warn the customer, and perhaps call in outside help. Your boss relies on you for information, however unpleasant.

● *Anticipated problems* You are often better able to foresee problems than is your boss, so make sure that you give adequate advance warnings.

● *Suggestions about work method changes* These may come from you or your subordinates. Remember to give credit to whoever thought up the bright idea, and try to *sell* it if it is a good one. Choose the right time to broach the subject, when your manager is not too busy, and support the idea with facts and figures. If possible put it down on paper. It strengthens your case if you can show savings over a period of months. It is not enough to put up your ideas and leave the boss to do all the spadework on them. Think through the snags and find the answers to possible objections so that the idea does not have to be shelved pending further information being obtained.

It will pay you to let the matter rest if you are getting nowhere. The seed of your idea may develop and bear fruit later. Provided nobody forgets whose idea it was, the delay may not matter.

Table 10.1 Checklist on communication (upwards and downwards)

Questions	✗✓	*Notes*
1. Do you know all of your subordinates by name?		
2. Do they all clearly know who their boss is?		
3. Do you know who yours is? Do you sometimes feel you have two bosses?		
4. Do your employees know the reasons for the jobs which they are asked to do? Not simply being told 'because the boss says so'.		
5. Are you able to introduce changes in your work group without major upsets?		
6. Do you manage to deal with problems and so avoid their being brought up through the union?		

Questions	×✓	Notes
7. Do you take up ideas put forward by the staff and secure action on them or explain why they cannot be acted upon?		
8. Do you consult those nearest the job on matters affecting the work?		
9. Do you take your subordinate supervisors into your confidence?		
10. Are you careful about the introduction of new employees to see that they quickly become members of the working team?		
11. Do all your subordinates know what their jobs are?		
12. Are there no dangerous rumours in circulation?		
13. Do your subordinate supervisors seldom get bypassed in the flow of information?		
14. Do you?		
15. Do you take up on subordinates' behalf questions which they have raised with you but which you cannot answer?		
16. Do your employees show a sustained interest in their jobs?		
17. Does the department function smoothly without staff constantly coming to you for information which they ought to have been given?		
18. Do you often go round your department (once a day at least)?		
19. Are you available enough?		

Questions

1. If an acquaintance complained that the shop stewards were not explaining company policy to the employees in a particular company, how would you correct this viewpoint?
2. How is morale affected by the standard of communication within the organization?
3. How can management ensure that there is a full interchange of information at all levels?
4. Why is good communication so important in a company?
5. Is the grapevine an advantage to a company? Please give reasons.
6. What are the main reasons for failure of communication in a company? Consider organizational problems, attitude problems and method problems.
7. Give your views on joint consultation.

11. *The supervisor's responsibility for safety*

Every supervisor must be concerned with the safety of his or her staff for three main reasons:

The humanitarian reason
This is a straightforward responsibility to other people for the safety of their life and limb. The statistics in Britain are:

Every year

550 people are killed
300 000 are injured
6 per cent of these are boys and girls under 18—a very high percentage when you consider what a small fraction of the workforce is in that age group.

Each injury means suffering to the individual, possible incapacity, loss of earnings, and hardship to the family.

The legal responsibility
The law makes it obligatory for a company to provide safe working conditions and insists on the use of safe working methods. Cases are on record of supervisors themselves being fined for contravening the law in this respect.

The economic reason
Accidents and industrial diseases cost very much more than the

cheques for compensation and fines. Often there is material damage, as in the case of a factory fire. Then there is the cost of lost work, perhaps increased by failure to meet production deadlines and, possibly, by the loss of customer goodwill. There is a loss of time in the investigation of the accident, and in people giving evidence or talking about it, spoilt material and damaged tools. There are many hidden losses too; a shop where there are accidents is not a happy workplace, and low morale will always affect people's job-enthusiasm and therefore their productivity. The economic reason alone is a powerful enough one to justify every effort to keep down accidents.

Many firms have a safety officer, and supervisors sometimes make the mistake of thinking that safety is really the *specialist's* business, not theirs. In fact, of course, it is *everybody's* business, but the one who can do most to prevent accidents is the supervisor.

The safety department's task is to help managers and supervisors in their job of getting the work done safely. They give advice, keep meaningful statistics on accidents for management's and supervisors' guidance, lend their weight to pressure for safer working conditions, and provide accident prevention aids like non-slip stickers, reflectors, guards and safety posters.

The safety officer normally has no more authority on the shopfloor than one manager has in another's department. Authority is not usually given to hold up production and tell a person to do the job in another way. The safety officer would preferably advise the employee's superior immediately. In an emergency, of course, commonsense should prevail. Anyone seen smoking in an oil refinery could rightly be reprimanded immediately by anybody in authority, or by any fellow-worker for that matter.

It is logical that you cannot normally have safety officers crossing the lines of authority, issuing orders and reprimands, and equally logical that they cannot be held responsible for the individual unsafe acts of all workers. The supervisors have this responsibility and the safety officer helps them to fulfil it.

How can you promote safety in your department?

Set a good example

Actions speak louder than words. It is important that you show in everything you do that your motto is 'Safety First'. Although you may be 100 per cent sure you could do something unsafe and get away with it, you must refrain from doing so because of the bad example you will be setting to others.

Always plan safety into every job by anticipating the potential hazards

Suppose you have a cleaner/maintenance operator in your section and you want some light fittings in the ceiling in your area cleaned outside working hours, as this is the most convenient time. There is a 15-foot high stepladder, self supports, and the ceiling is 18 feet high. What do you think are the potential hazards, and how would you prevent them resulting in an accident?

Table 11.1 shows what you should consider:

Table 11.1 Potential hazard avoidance

Potential hazard	Plan of action
Electric shock	Ensure lights are switched off and alternative lighting is available
Ladder collapses	Check it for safety
Light fitting could fall	Tell cleaner not to remove it
Operator could be injured erecting and moving the ladder	Extra man needed
Light fitting could be loosened during cleaning, and might fall	Ask the operator to report any defects in the fittings to you

Insist that people do things the safe way

It may sound like nagging, and you may be reluctant to make a nuisance of yourself, but remember that all employees will respect you more for your interest in their safety.

Here is the recommended procedure for correcting an employee who has not been observing the laid-down safety rules. (It can be short-circuited if the employee has acted so dangerously that you should classify the offence as 'serious industrial misconduct', such as smoking in an oil refinery.)

1. Check that the system of working and the equipment concerned are really adequate and satisfactory.
2. Consider whether the equipment or system of work requires redesigning, either to remove employees' objections or so as to make it impossible for the machine or equipment to be used in the dangerous manner complained of.
3. Train, instruct and supervise the employee in the use of the system and/or equipment.
4. Consult any workers' organization or committee, establishing that they fully understand the arrangements and approve of them—and seek their help in the enforcement of the rules and in remonstrating with non-complying employees.
5. Speak personally to the employee who is not complying with the rules; emphasize the importance of doing so, and give due warning of the consequences of failure.
6. Refer the employee to sections 7 and 8 of the Health and Safety at Work Act 1974, which require employees to take proper care for their own safety and not to interfere with safety equipment—and which render them liable to the same penalties for breach as the employing company or managers.
7. If the oral request to reform fails, deliver a written one, preferably by hand. If possible obtain a signed receipt acknowledging the warning.
8. If danger (actual or potential) is being caused to fellow employees, emphasize the unfairness of the conduct to others.

9. If the dangerous behaviour persists, consider dismissal. Factors to be taken into account include:
   (a) the nature and extent of the danger—to the employee concerned and to others;
   (b) the effect of dismissal on good industrial relations;
   (c) the employee's length of service, degree of responsibility and general conduct; and
   (d) all the other circumstances of the case which might make the dismissal 'unfair', so as to give the employee a right to compensation.
10. Collate your documentation—including records of efforts to persuade the employee to take care and discussions with safety representatives, trade unions and/or fellow workers.
11. Deliver a second written warning, stating:
   (a) if applicable, that further non-compliance will leave you with no alternative other than to dismiss and in any event
   (b) drawing the employee's attention to previous warnings; to the Health and Safety at Work Act and rules thereunder; and stating that no responsibility can in any case be accepted for injury, loss or damage to the employee. (But note: although this disclaimer may be of help in a civil action it will not necessarily free the employers from liability.)

You may wish to alter the order in which these steps are listed so that the sequence suits your business or the particular circumstances. But if you follow this general outline it can hardly be said that you did not take reasonable steps to correct the employee concerned.

In the event of an accident you would probably avoid liability since you would have drawn the employee's attention to the dangers and done everything you could to avoid them.

In your inspection tours, make a point of checking on safety matters

Look at the checklists at the end of this chapter to remind

MAKE A POINT OF
CHECKING ON SAFETY MATTERS

yourself of some of the things to look for. Write in other points that matter in your job.

Be insistent towards management about points of safety

One works manager told a group of managers and foremen at a conference that they must make a nuisance of themselves in his office if they ever thought a safety point was being overlooked in spite of repeated reminders. Managers have to respond to pressures from customers and superiors to get production out. They cannot do their job properly unless people below them have the courage to put with equal insistence the need for safe practices.

Investigate accidents to prevent recurrences

All accidents should be investigated, whether or not an injury or damage resulted. An accident is any *unplanned event*. Perhaps as many as nine out of ten accidents do not result in an injury, but the one that does is only the tip of the iceberg.

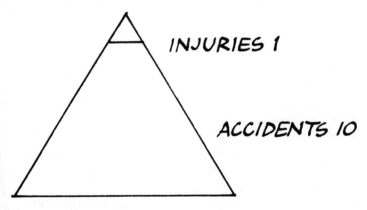

Figure 11.1 The accident iceberg

Suppose you are chopping wood and the head flies off the axe, burying itself in the grass. You must regard this as an accident, diagnose its cause, and prevent a recurrence. You were just lucky that nobody was hurt on this occasion.

If an accident occurs, find out who and what caused it. Don't make the mistake of thinking that accidents just happen. Every accident is caused by something which somebody does, or fails to do. Track down the cause and ensure that it will never happen again.

Provide protecting clothing

Protective clothing does not stop an accident happening but it can minimize the injury. Simply by putting on a pair of goggles a grindstone operator is not prevented from having an accident. To do that the operator must be sure that the stone is not cracked, that it is being run at the right number of revs, and used for the right purpose. But protective clothing is a safeguard.

Remember the special problems of your older workers

Taking this to mean people over 55, there are certain factors which must be considered in assigning work to them. Age may bring wisdom but it does not always bring sufficient self-knowledge for individuals to know what they can and can no longer do.

There are many older people who are more alert than 20-year-olds, but on the whole they tend to have slower reactions, a less ready grasp of new work techniques and less accurate sight and hearing. Some may have a tendency to dizziness or drowsiness, a greater tendency to falling and a greater susceptibility to injury when doing so.

These factors should not deter you from employing or continuing to employ older men and women. Often their experience and proven loyalty more than outweigh the drawbacks, but the shortcomings must be reckoned with in spite of the fact that many people conceal their disabilities because they are afraid of the consequences of complaining. Here are some safety tips for dealing with older people on the job:

- See that the lighting is adequate and provide more if necessary.
- Give them less arduous work.
- Provide seats if possible.

- Observe their particular weak points, and avoid placing them in jobs in which their handicaps could be a danger to themselves and others.

Young people have problems too

Newcomers to industry have their own problems of adjustment. They are probably unused to the hazards of the shopfloor, with heavy, noisy, dangerous machinery. They are usually inexperienced at the job, anxious not to appear timid, unaccustomed to the monotony of some types of work which require constant vigilance, and perhaps inclined to high spirits and horseplay.

The accident prone

Safety records show that accidents happen more frequently to a small number of employees and that most never have any at all. The few who are most frequently involved are known as *accident prone*. Often their susceptibility to accidents is the result of inadequate training or high work pressure. Perhaps the working environment is particularly dangerous. A few accident-prone people are inclined that way because of some psychological state—something in their character which makes them try to evade the rules, buck the system, not only on the job but in everything they do. It may be something which gives them a tendency to self-injury or self-destruction; perhaps just a lackadaisical attitude to life in general.

Accident-prone people must be identified and, in the first instance, drilled in safe ways of working. The ultimate resort— a change of jobs—may have to be faced in extreme cases which do not respond to other remedies.

Run your own safety meetings

When some potential source of accident becomes apparent, it is a good idea to call the team together round a machine, outline the problem and ask for suggestions. There may be no specific hazard but you may wish to have a general discussion about safety to bring the matter to the forefront of their minds. By asking for their suggestions you enlist their support for your safety objectives without thereby losing any of your authority, because the last word is always with you.

Your union representative will be glad to lend support, for in the matter of safety you share the same objectives. Quite apart from its value as an accident prevention measure, this will very probably pave the way for greater cooperation and understanding on other issues too.

Cooperate with your safety representatives

The Health and Safety at Work Act 1974 requires the appointment of *safety representatives* who have the following responsibilities:

- To inspect for safe premises, tools and working practices.
- To investigate accidents.
- To form part of the establishment's Safety Committee.

They help the company to prevent accidents by:

- Adding weight to the company's own safety programme.
- Influencing their fellow workers.
- Adding their own vigilance to yours.
- Reminding you of the need for accident prevention.

Your safety representative has his own important role, so make sure you know who he or she is, and exactly what their powers are in your company.

How safety-minded are you?

Table 11.2 shows a checklist which you can use to improve your own standards.

Table 11.2 Checklist on safety

Questions	✗ ✓
1. Do you ensure that unskilled staff in your section do not practise using dangerous machinery without expert guidance?	
2. Are the right tools provided?	
3. Do you ensure that they are kept in good condition?	
4. Are the appropriate people assigned to potentially dangerous jobs?	
5. Do you ensure that staff do not take unsafe short cuts?	
6. Are machines fitted with the necessary guards and are they in good working order?	
7. Do you ensure that guards are used?	
8. Are machines switched off when not in use?	
9. Does your department *condition* staff to safety?	
10. Do your staff show safety-consciousness?	
11. Are they well informed about potential hazards?	
12. Do you stress safety during the induction of new staff?	
13. Are new staff alerted to local dangers?	
14. Do you ensure correct handling and lifting methods are used?	
15. Have those staff who have to lift heavy or awkward loads received training in manual lifting and handling?	
16. Are there proper emergency drills and are these known?	
17. Do you arrange refresher safety training?	
18. Do you ensure that your staff are trained to use the correct signals?	
19. Do you ever give your staff pep talks on safety?	
20. Is there a planned maintenance programme?	
21. Is maintenance safely carried out, in your opinion?	
22. Are adequate isolation switches used?	

The supervisor's responsibility for safety 133

Table 11.2 *(continued)*

Questions	✗✓

23. Do you ensure that correct methods are used in slinging loads?
24. Would you stop production to make something safe?
25. Have you considered painting the guards a conspicuous colour?
26. Do you thoroughly know your plant?
27. In planning a job, do you make the safety angle an important part of your plan, anticipating dangers?
28. Have you ever arranged a safety competition for your staff?
29. Do you ensure that you have enough help for a dangerous job?
30. Do you and your staff know the safety regulations and the reasons behind them?
31. Are you strict about safety?
32. Do you arrange for automatic safety devices to be fitted when possible?
33. Do you try to avoid distractions?

Fire

1. Do you know and observe the fire regulations? Does everybody in your department?
2. Do you have the extinguishers you need?
3. Have you recently held a fire practice?
4. Is there an adequate alarm system?
5. Is your firefighting equipment regularly tested?
6. Are you strict about smoking only in prescribed areas?
7. Are these clearly defined?
8. Do you know the position of the fire exits and are they kept clear?
9. Do you and your staff know how to use the extinguishers?

10. Are the fire doors kept free at all times (i.e. not propped open or blocked)?
11. In the event of fire could you be sure that everybody was out of the building?

Electrical dangers

1. Are electrical installations safe, especially temporary ones?
2. Are all points, AC and DC, clearly marked?
3. Are power tools working off a low voltage with a transformer?
4. Do you avoid the misuse of electrical equipment?
5. Do you know where the main switches are?
6. Is a competent person nominated for electrical maintenance in the department?
7. Are the cables and leads properly insulated, and not frayed, worn, bared or perished?

First aid

1. Do you insist on prompt first aid for injuries?
2. Do you have a trained 'first aider' and do you both have access to an adequate first-aid box?
3. Do the staff know where to go if first aid is needed?

General

1. Do you practise what you preach about safety?
2. Do you consider your own health and safety?
3. Is there good discipline (absence of horseplay)?
4. Is there adequate protective clothing?
5. Do you see that people use it?
6. Do you encourage people to report hazards?
7. Do you act promptly on these reports?

Table 11.2 (*continued*)

Questions	✗ ✓
8. Do you investigate accidents to prevent recurrences?	
9. Do you arrange an adequate follow-up on this?	
10. Do you know and observe any legal requirements concerning the materials and machines you supervise?	
11. Has your department a good safety record?	
12. Do you continually consider what you can do to improve it?	
13. Do you have proper storage facilities for dangerous materials?	
14. Have you adequate safety posters?	
15. Is there a clearly defined place for safety equipment?	
16. Are barrier creams supplied where necessary?	
17. Do you encourage safety suggestions and is there a recognized channel for these?	
18. Do you avoid dangerously long hours?	
19. Do you guard against fatigue risks?	
20. Do you guard against stress endangering any employee?	
21. Do employees know whom they must contact at all times in case of an accident?	
22. Is there adequate protective clothing, and does *everybody*, including visitors, use it?	
23. Do you report accident statistics to your team?	
24. Are there clear markings to identify the correct stacking areas?	
25. Are stacks safe?	
26. Has the layout of your workplace been planned with safety in mind?	
27. Is there adequate space between machines?	
28. Do you arrange an adequate check-up after installation?	
29. Are steam pipes safely covered?	
30. Are compressed air or pressure vessels regularly tested?	

Questions	✗ ✓
31. Have you arranged for safety glass to be fitted where advisable?	
32. Are poisonous materials properly supervised?	
33. Are pipes correctly colour-coded?	
34. Are accidents publicized to prevent recurrences?	
35. Do you know the Health and Safety at Work Act and Regulations as they affect you?	
36. Do you ensure unauthorized entry is prevented?	
37. Is there emergency lighting?	
38. Are there adequate warning signals?	
39. Have you an easy reference for the telephone numbers of the fire brigade and the medical department or doctor?	
40. Do you consult your union representative on safety?	
41. Do you insist on rules about no running?	
42. Do the emergency stop buttons work properly?	

Inspection

1. Do you keep your eyes open for hazards?
2. Is the workplace tidy?
3. Is the lighting adequate?
4. Are the gangways and exits kept clear?
5. Are hazards eliminated or clearly marked?
6. Are the floors safe (e.g., no slippery substances on floor, ruts eliminated, pits properly covered)?
7. If you use footboards are they in a safe condition?
8. Do you ensure that transport and lifting tackle are safe?
9. Do you ask to see the Factory Inspectors' reports?
10. Are openings roped off or otherwise safeguarded?
11. Are the safety regulations displayed?
12. Are staff safely dressed?
13. Are safe working loads observed?
14. Are there safe ladders and staging?

Questions

1. Give the outline of a safety talk which you would deliver to your staff at the start of Safety Week in your organization.
2. Annual reports of the Chief Inspector of Factories show that approximately 20 per cent of all accidents are caused by incorrect handling and lifting of goods. You are the safety officer of an engineering factory. Your directors have noticed the latest reports and have asked you to outline the steps that you propose taking to ensure that such accidents are reduced to the lowest possible figures. Draft your proposals in a report.
3. You are walking through a department which is not your own and you see an employee doing his job with the safety guard off his machine. What can you do?
4. As a supervisor how can you foster safety-consciousness among staff and enlist their cooperation in reducing accidents?
5. 'Safety is the safety officer's job.' Why is this statement misleading and potentially dangerous?
6. What would you do if an employee were negligent about wearing eye protection? What would be your next step if he took little notice?
7. What would you do if an employee had a spate of accidents?
8. A sling securing a load of one ton breaks and the load falls six feet to the ground. Nobody is injured and no damage results. Has an accident happened?
9. In a materials department a stockchecker wanted to check the contents of a bin on a 14-foot-high shelf. He persuaded a fork-lift truck driver to put two planks on the forks to make a platform for him to stand on. When he reached the shelf he lost his balance, fell, and was killed. The supervisor was not in the department at the time. When the case came up whom do you think the court held to blame?

12. *Your union representative and you*

Trade unions have an important and constructive part to play in industry. Although management and employees have a common purpose in their work, there will always be a degree of contention about how to divide the income and about injustices, real or imagined, which arise in the process of earning it.

Unions can be a help to management and are likely to act moderately if the company has made genuine efforts to create a happy working environment through good communication, good terms and conditions, adequate attention to safety, health and welfare, and an equitable wage and salary structure. Where there is a union the company would be well advised to acknowledge its role in a positive way and do everything possible to encourage an open and mutually confident approach.

Properly established and recognized, a trade union can help management in the following ways:

- It can provide management with a coherent and unified workforce with which to negotiate.

- It can reassure employees that justice has been done, by supporting mutually agreed compromises.

- It can ventilate and express grievances which might otherwise fester away unnoticed and ultimately induce paralysis, because discontented staff do not work efficiently.

- It can build morale.

The union representative's job

There are about 200 000 representatives in British industry. The majority of them are dedicated people doing a difficult and often thankless job without any reward except the satisfaction of being of service. Representatives are in an awkward position. They are paid by management, to whom they sometimes look like deliberate agitators; elected by the staff, who sometimes suspect them of being management stooges; and they are under the vigilance of the trade union, with whose rules they are expected to conform even when they apparently oppose the staff's short-term needs. They have to safeguard each member's individual interests, while preserving the trade union legacy of which they are the main custodians. Yet they must help to preserve the company's prosperity which alone can guarantee the jobs of those who elected them. They spend on average 11 hours a week of company time on union business and five hours of their own leisure time. Their authority depends on the confidence they can win and maintain among the union's rank and file members, and they can only survive if they have a strong character, calmness and plenty of commonsense.

These are the groundrules for helping them—and you—to keep the peace

Don't use them as your mouthpiece

It is a mistake to use shop stewards as *your line of communication* in conveying messages to your employees, whether these are purely informational or whether they are warnings about lateness or other infractions. It is not the steward's job to communicate on management's behalf, but rather to protect the staff's interests. These cannot be put across to them with enthusiasm or conviction if they are policies or instructions with which the steward may later have to disagree. Management must do its own communicating and the logical way of going about this is to tell the supervisors who will then pass it on to all of their subordinates.

Keep them informed

If they know what is going on and what your plans are they can calm down members who come to them with exaggerated rumours and suspicions.

Consult them

Try not to react defensively when your staff offer an opinion, or to say, or think 'Are they trying to tell me how to do my job?' It is no reflection on your leadership if you consult them or the shop steward when you propose taking action on a matter which affects their interests. If you are going to make changes or take an unusual course of action you will find it much easier with prior consultation. You still have the last word, but they will appreciate having been asked their views.

Courtesy always pays

Give your shop stewards your undivided attention for a few minutes each day, and keep personalities out of the encounter. Inevitably the union representative will bring up more problems than other staff, but this should not prejudice you against the holder of that very difficult office.

Example

One transport department supervisor used to talk over cases with his shop steward in the presence of his chargehand and a clerk, and consequently felt he always had to put on an act and assert his authority. The shop steward said that if he could catch him in the yard and go and sit with him in the quiet of one of the driving cabs, he became quite a different person— reasonable, calm, and prepared to admit he might be wrong.

Everybody always has to act slightly differently when a third person is present, so if you think an audience could spoil your interview, conduct it in private. Ask the clerk to look after the telephone. Sometimes in a tense situation you will need to have someone present as a witness, but it should be possible to have off-the-record communication as well.

If you have to give a severe reprimand, try to have the shop steward there

It is natural enough for anybody who is smarting under a reprimand to present a biased account when telling the story to a representative. Often the representative hears conflicting stories about what happened—the supervisor says one thing and the employee another. If the representative is present when you issue your warning you will find that he or she is in a much better position to deal fairly with the case, and will not be deceived by an incomplete account of the facts.

Learn the procedure and observe it

If you break with procedure you will weaken any case which may arise and unnecessarily damage your relationship with the representative.

Learn the rules and observe them

Unless you do you will create problems for yourself and the shop steward, who probably has to contend with at least one barrack-room lawyer among the membership.

Have a good working knowledge of employer–employee law

Don't leave the representative to handle all complaints and grievances

If you regard the steward as an unofficial welfare officer in the department you may lose personal contact with your team. Encourage individuals to come straight to you with their grievances. The representative is there to give support to an individual only if the supervisor is unable to give an answer which satisfies the person concerned.

Don't delegate the compiling of rotas (e.g. overtime, shiftwork, holidays) to the steward

This is part of supervision, and needs to be done with a sound knowledge of job requirements. Moreover, if an employee is dissatisfied with the rota and the shop steward is the one who organized it, there is nobody else to appeal to.

Try to see ways round restrictive practices

Restrictive practices are arrangements which were originally meant to protect people's jobs and levels of income. Today they do not always make sense and can result in overmanning, wasteful job demarcations, unnecessary overtime and sheer boredom and frustration, all of which put up costs and sap enthusiasm. When this happens it is a direct threat to the security of the company and everyone employed there. The shop stewards have little choice but to abide by the rules, and it is no good trying to force them to abandon this kind of custom. When you see such practices impeding efficiency, sound out the shop steward's views and then try to suggest to your superior ways in which the work could be carried out more logically. This could be just the kind of bargaining point which the company is looking for in the next round of negotiations.

Know the union

If you know the union rules, its structure, who has the power, and when officials are due to come up for re-election, you will understand the attitudes of the people you are dealing with. For example, an official whose term of office is expiring and who wants to be re-elected can be an uncompromising bargainer. It will probably pay the company to postpone any negotiations until after the voting.

Conclusion

Your shop steward must play his or her part in representing the employees of the company, just as the buyer represents the market and the board of directors represents the shareholders. In order to negotiate in an enlightened way and to do the job with a sense of responsibility, the union representative needs *recognition* and *information*. You can play your part in seeing that he or she receives both, and can appreciate why management sometimes unintentionally makes the mistake of giving more of these two commodities to the union than to you.

Table 12.1 Checklist on working with your union representative

Questions	✗ ✓	*Notes*
1. Do you avoid asking the representative to make announcements to the staff on your behalf?		
2. Do you keep him or her informed of your intentions?		
3. Are you good at passing on to him or her those items of information which top managment wish you to?		
4. Do you consult the representative on matters concerning the staff?		
5. Do you treat him or her as courteously as you would a fellow supervisor?		
6. Do you consider whether to have the representative in attendance when you issue a reprimand?		
7. Do you know and observe the procedure?		
8. Do you know and observe the rules and agreements?		
9. Do you know your company's policy on union membership?		
10. Do you know your company's policy on allowing union representatives to deal with union business during working hours?		

Questions	✗✓	Notes
11. Do you know and use the agreed grievance procedure and disciplinary procedure?		
12. Do you know whether you have the authority to reprimand, suspend or dismiss?		
13. Does the representative know and adhere to grievance procedure?		
14. Have you read the Code of Industrial Relations Practice (Her Majesty's Stationery Office)?		
15. Do you know employer–employee law sufficiently well to keep out of trouble?		

Questions

1. How can the supervisor and union representative best work together for the good of the company and the employees of the department?
2. It is said that management gets the sort of shop steward it deserves. Discuss this statement.

13. *Don't do it all yourself*

DON'T DO IT ALL YOURSELF

Are you a supervisor or a superworker? The supervisor's job is to plan, organize, coordinate the work within a department and the department's work with the rest of the organization, to give instructions and ensure that output is being maintained according to plan. Like the captain of a ship you should be in overall control. Nobody is going to be impressed if the skipper is setting a good example in the galley or engine room and neglecting the bridge.

WHO'S ON THE BRIDGE ?

The most effective managers and supervisors are those who spend their time doing accurately and effectively the task which only they can do, not everybody else's work. Yet you will hear them say, 'I could do it more quickly myself than if I stop to explain.' 'We are short-handed. I have to let some of my jobs go by the board while I give a hand on production.' This seems an easy way out. Production usually does not need as much thought as supervision, and it is sometimes a sign of subconsciously dodging the real job.

It is also a shortsighted view. If you take the trouble to explain the job, others will know how to do it next time. If you aren't getting the work out, could it be because staff aren't receiving proper supervision?

Example

In a stone quarry one of the more difficult and dangerous (but fortunately infrequent) jobs consists of abseiling down the quarry face and dislodging dangerous outcrops. One quarry manager used to do this personally, probably as a kind of ritual. But what does it prove? Is retirement the only answer when this feat is no longer possible? Obviously not, since organizing and leadership ability can outlast physical prowess. Such activities have been called 'occupational hobbies'. Be careful not to indulge yourself for more than 5 per cent of the time on yours.

Delegating duties

Many supervisors find that they can go further than simply keeping their hands off the work which their staff ought to handle—they can actively delegate. This means giving somebody below you a job which you used to do yourself, or would have done yourself, and allowing that person to finish it without hindrance. This is not always easy and you obviously cannot go against trade union regulations or overload somebody who already has too much work. When you let subordinates make *decisions* you not only relieve yourself of the thinking (though not of the responsibility), but can actually alleviate the workload of the person delegated to. You eliminate delays while they wait for your answers, and you develop their capabilities and powers of judgement. Most welcome the chance of using more discretion in their jobs and the increased self-confidence, understanding and experience they gain. Some may ask for more money if a great deal of work is delegated; if they deserve it, and it is feasible, why not? It may pay to have fewer, more capable staff with higher wages than twice as many people who cannot do much without their supervisor's help.

What duties can you start delegating? Write down everything you have to do in the course of your work. Do not put in too much detail. Table 13.1 gives an example:

Table 13.1   Work delegation plan

What I do	*Who can do it now?*	*Who could do it when trained?*
Allocate jobs to sections in conjunction with section heads	—	
Check samples for quality	All section supervisors	
Order materials for whole department	—	J. Clifford, section supervisor
Recommend salary adjustments	All section supervisors	
Show Safety Inspector around department	L. Rogers, section supervisor	
Call in service department in case of breakdown	All section supervisors	
Plan departmental training programme for apprentices		Section supervisors

You should have three columns in all. The first is headed 'What I do', the second, 'Who can do it now?', and the third, 'Who could do it when trained?' When you systematically consider how to pass these duties down the line you may be able to offload a quarter of your day-to-day worries immediately. Others can be allocated when the people you think could be trained to help you are ready to do so. You will probably need to let your superior know of your delegation plans and obtain approval, and of course it will be made clear that the responsibility still remains yours.

Begin by delegating duties which recur. Usually they are routine, not too difficult and, because of their frequency, take up most time. Then you can probably delegate those items which you personally are least qualified to handle if you have an employee who is something of an expert. There is no disgrace in one of your staff being able to do a job better than you. The higher one is promoted, the more this is likely to be the case.

Some kinds of jobs can be delegated mainly as a means of training.

Ask yourself:

- 'What kind of experience do I want to give each of these people in order to develop their full value to the enterprise?'
- 'What could I delegate that is related to the job they are already doing?'
- What duties can I delegate which have a satisfying and evident result when properly completed?'
- 'What duties can I delegate to particular people in view of their special aptitudes and inclinations, thereby ensuring that they will be carried through willingly?'
- 'What can I delegate which will give people the right amount of challenge?'
- 'What sequence of delegations can I arrange so that each of my staff achieves a series of successes?'

Here are some useful tips to help you in carrying through your programme of delegation.

Delegate the thinking and decision making as well as the doing
You are not delegating unless you leave sufficient discretionary powers to the person who has to do the job. In some of the best-run firms, from the managing director downwards, decisions are taken at the lowest possible level. The policy that underlies all decisions is formulated at the top and communicated downwards so that everybody knows what it is and why it is so.

Tie in training with delegation You learn from your mistakes, of course, but too many errors can be demoralizing. So explain things clearly to subordinates before you delegate. Once they have mastered the essentials, you can delegate progressively harder jobs which will in themselves be a form of training. To protect yourself and them against their own inexperience let them start by making decisions on matters which would not disrupt the whole works if they went wrong.

Delegate the right to be wrong Any work decision is based on knowledge and experience which may produce two or three alternative solutions to the problem in hand. The final decision is a matter of discretion—often a question of weighing each alternative and selecting the best. If people to whom you have delegated jobs have enough knowledge and experience, but in weighing the alternatives make a different choice from yours, resist the temptation to interfere. If you don't, they will form the habit of checking back constantly and relying too heavily on your advice.

Stand by their decisions and accept responsibility for them
Supervision is a tough job. It looks as though your subordinates will get the credit if a project turns out well and you will be blamed if it fails. Some supervisors keep a card on their desk inscribed 'The buck stops here'. There is no doubt that all supervisors and managers are responsible for the actions of their subordinates and it could not be otherwise, but managers do not usually overlook the fact that good results from the team mean good supervision. If one of your staff makes a mistake,

Don't do it all yourself 151

back up the person, even if the decision itself cannot be justified, and accept overall responsibility. Your subordinate will save face if allowed to rectify the error personally, and you can avoid stepping in.

Encourage people to think through their own problems   You can do this by turning people's questions back to them and asking them for their ideas on how a given problem should be solved.

Don't delegate overlapping jobs to separate people unless this is specifically recognized   Nobody likes to find that somebody else has been working on the job which he or she has been given. It seems to show a lack of trust.

Try to distribute your delegated work   Arrange for as many people as possible to take decisions. By giving everybody a chance you will spread the advantages and risks and not overload one person.

Make individuals' authority clear   If you give staff members responsibility you must ensure that they have enough authority for carrying it through. So make sure that other people whose help will be needed know that they have been given the job.

Consider when to delegate   When you are assigned a new employee, when a system is changed, or when a new job comes up—these are all good opportunities. Make a start now with your list of duties and begin offloading from today.

Delegate gradually   It may take a year to delegate all you can, so don't rush it.

Be patient   When you start delegating you will find that your workload is greater, because you have to train, guide and correct the employees to whom you are assigning the work. Once you have made the effort to do this, however, you begin to reap cumulative rewards.

Work towards a system of 'management by exception' This means that your staff do not waste your time reporting about those things which are going normally, but only those things which are exceptions—whether good or bad. Provided the system is working properly you know that no news means everything is normal. There is no failsafe on this, so you do have to check the really important issues periodically. The morning inspection is as good a time as any.

Don't be a constant 'checker-upper' Decide how you are going to appraise results, but remember how it feels to have someone constantly at your elbow watching you. Leave your staff to get on with the job.

DON'T BE A CONSTANT 'CHECKER-UPPER'

In order to find out if you are delegating enough, test yourself on the checklist shown in Table 13.2.

Table 13.2 Checklist on delegation

Questions	×✓	Notes
1. Are you seldom interrupted by staff asking you about the job, what, why, how and who is to do it?		
2. Do you have to decide all matters or do your staff have some power of decision making?		
3. Do you seldom find yourself doing the jobs of some of your staff when they really ought to be doing them themselves?		
4. Do you have time to plan your work and manage your staff properly?		
5. Are you good at organizing the job to be done and leaving the details to the one who is to do it?		
6. Do you avoid breathing down people's necks?		
7. Do you show confidence in your staff's ability?		
8. Do you avoid setting your standards so high that only you can attain them?		
9. Do you disclose details about the job, dispelling any unnecessary air of secrecy?		
10. How often do you allow your subordinates to do the thinking about a particular job as well as the doing?		
11. Do you always give enough information about the job so that if things go wrong those responsible can use their own initiative to put them right?		

Questions	x✓	Notes
12. Do your subordinate supervisors have access to procedure guides, rulebooks, etc., so that they can take action on their own?		
13. Do you avoid habitually working longer hours than the people under you?		
14. Are you seldom rushed off your feet?		
15. Do you delegate the right to be wrong?		
16. Do you ensure that there is full understanding between you and your subordinates about the requirements of the job?		
17. When you are away does the work go on normally?		
18. Is there good liaison between your department and others on delegated work?		
19. Have all the jobs been analysed and is each one being done by the right calibre person?		
20. Are the capabilities of each of your staff being fully used?		
21. Are there sufficient signatories and are the signing and authorization procedures efficient?		
22. Are the standardized form letters/memos up to date and are they being properly used?		

Questions

1. 'I could do it myself quicker than if I stopped to explain.' What is the fallacy of this argument if used too often?
2. Outline a programme for effective delegation within a department.

14. *The organization: working as a member of the management team*

Today many supervisors work within large and complex organizations and the supervisor is often no longer solely in charge of his department. There are planners, programmers, inspectors, progress chasers and large numbers of other specialists all having a say in how well, how soon, in what way, and at what cost, the product must be made. Sometimes it looks as though all these people are just passengers on the back of those who do the production job, but this is a false picture. To understand the function of all these specialists it is useful to identify three main kinds of activity in industry, namely:

- the deciding
- the systematic planning
- the doing.

In smaller companies top management does the deciding and lower management and the employees carry out the doing with as much planning as time permits. In larger organizations top management still does the deciding but the broad systematic planning is done by specialists so that lower management and the production staff can devote their full energies to production.

If supervisors are to work well, particularly in these new huge and complicated industrial concerns, it is important for them to understand something about principles of organization. All supervisors are practitioners in management and should know the theory of it if they are to do their job properly. For this reason, I should firstly like to outline the main features of a typical company and then talk about some of the problems which may arise in the course of its work.

The structure of the organization

The shareholders

If you buy shares in a company you become a member of it and are entitled to a share of the profits which it makes. Shareholders have an Annual General Meeting to receive the chairman's report on the year's activities and to express their views on this subject and about future policy.

The function of the shareholders is to criticize and review.

The board of directors

This is responsible for the conduct of the business and for broad policy decisions. The results of its discussions are usually put into effect through the medium of the chief executive or managing director. Sometimes, however, other directors are also given executive powers and are therefore known as 'executive directors'. They have the authority to give instructions directly to the managers below them without going through the managing director. The board's main function can be defined as one of policy making.

The management and operatives

The managing director is able to achieve production because overall responsibility is broken down into manageable parts given to managers, specialists, superintendents, supervisors, section heads and operators. There is no standard pattern of organization throughout industry—nothing to parallel the army's system—because one productive unit doesn't usually have to face the same problem in the same way as another.

The organization should be flexible, changing with the times and the new problems to be tackled. Too often businesses fail to do so due to short-sightedness or lack of courage in dealing with executives who have become firmly entrenched and resist change—restrictive practices are not only resorted to on the shop floor! To turn a blind eye to them at any level will only aggravate an already unsatisfactory situation.

Here are some typical organizational arrangements:

Line organization   As you can see from Fig. 14.1, under this arrangement orders all flow through the 'line' and each person can clearly see that he is responsible to only one superior.

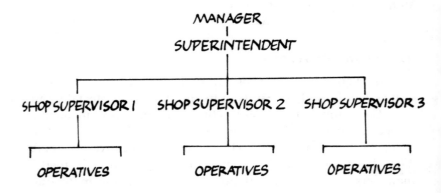

Figure 14.1 Line organization

Functional supervision   Towards the end of the last century managers were, in some industries, already beginning to realize that the job was becoming too complex for a foreman to deal with all the technical, specialists' problems which come up in a day's work. F. W. Taylor, an American machine shop manager, introduced a new system of control at the Midvale Steel Company of Philadelphia in 1882–3. The object was to divide the foreman's job into its different functions and have a supervisor for each. From the men's point of view, they had five supervisors, four responsible for special aspects and one 'gang boss'.

Taylor developed the idea further elsewhere into a plan like the one shown in Fig. 14.2.

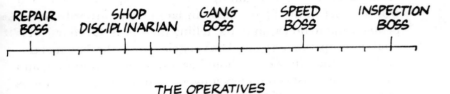

REPAIR BOSS   SHOP DISCIPLINARIAN   GANG BOSS   SPEED BOSS   INSPECTION BOSS

THE OPERATIVES

Figure 14.2 Functional supervision

There were, in addition to these supervisors, clerks responsible for the administrative work that has to go with production. Although Taylor says it worked well, the system has not survived to the present day in the same form. Many managers feel that if you have too many supervisors, each allowed to give instructions to the same group, and each holding them responsible, misunderstandings develop and tensions between the various executives with their different priorities will split workshop loyalties.

The 'line and staff' organization Under this plan only one supervisor is in charge of a particular group, but is supported and advised by specialists called staff officers. They do not carry any authority and cannot give orders (except to their own direct subordinates) but must work only through the medium of the supervisor, who weighs up the specialists' advice and decides whether to accept or reject it taking into account the complete picture.

The three arrangements outlined above suggest how authority and responsibility can be apportioned in an organization, and the most common system nowadays is a mixture of all three.

It is generally accepted (matrix management excluded—see page 164) that people cannot have more than one immediate superior and that if specialists are needed they should work through that person rather than give orders directly to the employees. However, sometimes specialist's advice is so crucial to the success of a particular operation, so unquestionable, that within strict limits he or she is in fact given authority to tell people what to do without first telling their boss. Of course, it is vital that supervisors should be very clear as to the extent of this authority, that this extent should be limited to a minimum, and that the specialist should never overstep it. If these precautions are taken, and provided you don't have too many functional specialists, it seems to work well. One good example of how it operates is when a ship's pilot takes over from the captain for a limited period and for the specific purpose of navigating a particular stretch of seaway or berthing the vessel.

Authority and responsibility

A football team would never go into action without being quite sure that the defence knew whom they were supposed to mark and what the goalkeeper and strikers were meant to be doing, but plenty of firms neglect to take similar precautions.

Many companies have improved the effectiveness of their executives and advisory staff by producing position descriptions. When people's jobs are clearly defined they are not afraid to take a step in case they tread on someone's toes, because everybody knows where they stand and what they are supposed to do.

Common weaknesses in companies' organization structures

Some companies are organizationally less efficient than they could be. Think of your own while you are reading this section. Identifying structural problems will help you to see the causes of some of your difficulties and where to watch your step.

Is the number of levels of authority kept to a minimum?

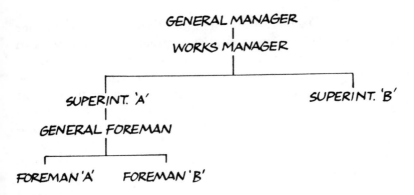

Figure 14.3 Levels of authority

If there are too many links in the chain of authority from the general manager to the shop floor (as shown in Fig. 14.3), the manager loses contact. More time is spent relaying messages, it takes longer to give decisions, and there seems to be less freedom of action because everything is decided somewhere up the line.

Whenever changes have to be made in work specifications or priorities, a long chain of command tends to make it harder to communicate. Staff soon feel despondent because they are so far removed from the top that they and their work does not seem to be in the limelight except for criticism. There is also the extra cost to the company of employing more administrators than are really necessary.

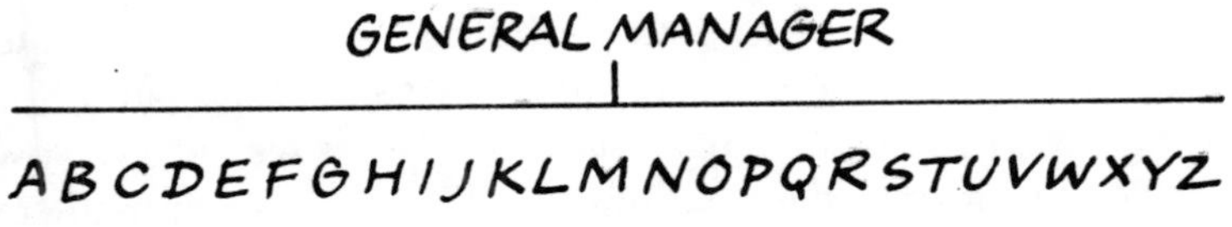

GENERAL MANAGER

A B C D E F G H I J K L M N O P Q R S T U V W X Y Z

Figure 14.4 Too wide a span of control

Have managers or supervisors too many people to supervise?

A number of widely different or unrelated jobs coming under the control of one manager will make greater demands than an equal number of similar ones would. But there is also clearly a limit to the number of even similar jobs one can supervise directly. Although there is no fixed number of people one person can supervise there are some useful points which tell you when there are too many. Watch for these signs: poor communication; employees' suggestions and ideas being overlooked; employees feeling that the supervisor does not count for much with the next level up; the tendency for rifts to develop between supervisor and manager. The cause of these could be that somebody has too wide a span of control.

Are managers tied to a particular process or technical expertise?

There are a number of ways of dividing up responsibility among managers. Too often a department will specialize in one particular process. Each has its pet technical job and you cannot introduce anything new unless you set up another department. It is like a social club having a committee for darts, one for snooker, one for football and one for outings. Why not have a committee for indoor activities and one for outdoor activities? Then you could introduce new pastimes. The same principle applies to industry. Perhaps processes could be grouped together under one head, who need not be an expert in each technology within that group, but knows enough about all of them, and enough about delegating, to guide and encourage subordinate experts. This was done in a printing company— one manager for preparing the printing surface with all its variations of letterpress, litho, etc., and one responsible for putting the print on the paper, whatever press was used. Now when a new process comes along it will not be so difficult to introduce. The managers are already there to handle it and all they need to do is to recruit their staff and delegate.

Does the division of work bring similar jobs together or separate them?

When similar functions are grouped together, spans of control can be wider and time, manpower, machinery and materials can be saved. Has each department, for example, developed its own paint shop with a range of paints, stencils, brushes, cleaning materials and its own labour? Perhaps there could be one large paint shop?

How does the organization structure affect the work?

In some organizations authority is blurred, and two departments, sections, or operatives feel jointly responsible. In such cases the jobs could be looked at again under the headings:

Jobs now done	Problems arising	Organizational changes which might ease them

Does the organization provide for every major duty to be carried out?

Some do not. An important duty takes second place in many an executive's crowded day. What duties have been partly overlooked in your company? Quality control? Staff development? Public relations? What organizational changes could be made in order to provide for their being properly carried out? Although you personally may not be in a position to change the structure, you can recognize the need for this, put forward suggestions when asked, and make allowances where you identify the root cause of problems which affect your job.

Are there water-tight compartments and over-specialization?

Is your firm a company or a collection of departments which take an 'I'm all right Jack' attitude to everybody else? This sort of thing is bad for the firm as a whole, for the best interests of the company are not always served by acting in the best interests of one particular department. Try to see your section as a part of the whole.

The view from the shopfloor

It is usual to think of Jones, Smith, Brown and all the other names on the organization chart as being people who are helping the managing director. But you could think of it the other way round, starting with the people on the shopfloor who are actually making the product. For example, what support and help do the employees need in order to enable them to do their jobs better? What does everybody else do to help them? Is each one doing a full-time job which really puts power into the firm to make and sell its products, or has Parkinson's Law taken over?

Matrix management

Traditional forms of line, function and staff management may be cumbersome when the company is developing new products or services. Companies which are breaking new ground in this way often find it useful to establish project teams with team leaders. The team leader may be the person who is going to make the major contribution to the project, or the natural leader, or the person who is in closest touch with the existing or potential customer. The leadership of the team may change as the project moves from the research and development phase to the production phase.

If, for example, an aerospace company wishes to develop a new type of engine, the line, functional and staff set-up could require the involvement of all levels of management and slow matters down with numerous committees and the need for approval to be sought for the most minute details. On the other hand, by seconding diverse departmental members to a project team and making its leader accountable for results a company would stand a better chance of coming up with a viable product ahead of its competititors.

When a company has a number of project teams at work the arrangement is referred to as *matrix management.*

The traditional view is that 'a man cannot serve two masters' (a line boss and a project team leader) but those companies who have felt compelled to adopt matrix management divide responsibilities and authority as shown in Fig. 14.5.

The 'horizontal' responsibility of the project team leader is for the successful outcome of the project. The 'vertical' responsibility of the department head is for professional standards and the longer term career prospects of the people seconded to the project team. The team member has a dual responsibility— upwards to the department head and horizontally to the project team leader.

If you find yourself appointed as a team leader you will need to focus your attention on the management and progress of the project as well as making a technical contribution from your specialist background. The POLCC cycle mentioned in Chapter 1 will come into play and you will need to provide leadership, enthusiasm and motivation to your group. You will need to be able to run a meeting, put a case, use your interviewing

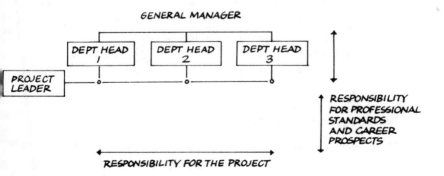

Figure 14.5 Matrix management

Working as a member of the management team 165

and listening skills, diagnose problems and make decisions. Your relationship with your team members' line managers will require tact, diplomacy and perhaps patience if matrix management is a new concept to them. Ultimately, if the company should eventually decide that it has to abandon the project for whatever commercial or other reason, you may have to do what the British officer couldn't do to the bridge he had built over the River Kwai. Project team leadership is an extremely demanding job; it is often the baptism of fire for the specialist who samples management for the first time, but in the final analysis it is the spearhead of innovation which as a nation we must have in order to survive.

If you are a line manager or supervisor who has temporarily seen one of your staff seconded to a project team, remember that you are that person's long-term anchor. Liaise with the project team leader when it comes to appraisal and career plans, and take an interest in his or her safety, health and welfare. Ensure that adequate training, support and updating in technology is available.

If you are a project team member you will have the satisfaction of working towards a specific goal—the successful outcome of the project. You will be the expert on your subject in that multidisciplinary team and you may have to do a balancing act between professionally correct procedures and the practical outcome of the project. As you will probably spend more time with your project team colleagues than your departmental boss, don't forget to keep the latter in the picture about what is going on, and draw on his or her experience when necessary.

Interdepartmental liaison

How good is cooperation between departments and shifts in your organization? Problems in this area are the most common of all now that rationalization, cut-backs, insecurity and change are in the air.

Example 1

In a round-the-clock production environment the components progressed through four departments via a series of conveyors, and operations were being performed at each of the four stages. The rivalry between shifts was so intense that when one shift found a way of increasing the flow by attaching a rubber band to strengthen a spring on the conveyor, they made a point of removing it before they handed over to their reliefs. This ensured that their production figures would always put them at the top of the shift production league table. The whole plant is now closed and production within the group of companies has been concentrated in other, more successful plants.

Example 2

In a warehousing and distribution company, the credit control department was threatening to sue a customer for non-payment of a supposedly outstanding bill. In fact the customer had returned the goods to the warehouse but the supervisor there had not advised the accounts department that a credit note should have been issued.

It is up to every supervisor to contribute to the improvement of interdepartmental cooperation as well as working at the relationships with his boss and subordinates. Interdepartmental cooperation is a key result area (see page 201) for all supervisors.

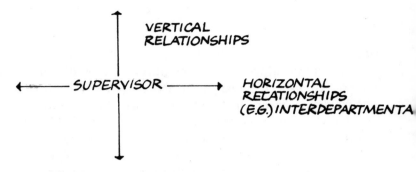

THE SUPERVISOR HAS TO DEVELOP HARMONIOUS
HORIZONTAL RELATIONSHIPS AS WELL AS VERTICAL ONES

**Figure 14.6 The supervisor must develop harmonious horizontal relationships
as well as vertical ones**

As you have no authority over your colleagues you have to win
their cooperation by giving them yours, and by knowing how to
be assertive without being aggressive. Let us take a closer look
at what this means.

Assertiveness means knowing what your rights are in a given
situation, while recognizing the rights of the person you are
dealing with.

Aggressiveness means going for your goals without regard for
the rights of the other person.

Non-assertiveness means allowing the other person to disregard
your rights.

For example, if you are approaching a junction where your
line of traffic merges with another, each stream having equal
rights:

Assertiveness means recognizing your opportunity and your
right to move into the merged line of traffic, and doing so
unwaveringly when there is no danger of collision.

Aggressiveness means going ahead regardless, so that the other line of traffic has to let you in or take the consequences.

Non-assertiveness means waiting until somebody in the other stream motions you to move in front (which could mean a long wait!).

Role conflict is natural and healthy

Role conflict, or differences of opinion between production and quality control, credit control and sales, maintenance and stores, accounts department and purchasing, etc., is natural and healthy because organizations, like individuals, can have dilemmas. Do we stock all possible spares even though we have to borrow to increase our working capital, or do we run on a shoestring and keep the bank happy? Do we make sure that the quality is perfect or do we go for production, facing the consequences that there may be a small number of customer complaints?

When an organization has a dilemma it may mean a clash of interests between managers or supervisors, but you must never let it become a clash of *personalities*. The production manager and quality control manager may frequently argue during working hours but should not allow this to affect their personal relationship.

Introduce new employees to their colleagues in other departments

When new people join your team make sure you introduce them to those whom they are going to be working with in other departments. This will stand them in good stead if potential problems arise.

Encourage a company-wide team spirit in your group

It is shortsighted to criticize other departments when talking with your team. Try to get them to see a broader perspective and to recognize the need for mutual respect and support.

Bear in mind that you are judged not only on your own performance but also on how well you work with the team

If you can sort out your problems at your own level so that you and your colleagues run a smooth operation, your boss will be able to concentrate his attention on breaking new ground instead of patching up rivalries.

Consider your colleagues' needs

Put yourself in their shoes. Abraham Maslow pointed out that each of us has five levels of need: first the basic survival needs, then safety, then belonging, next esteem, and finally self-fulfilment. These needs are usually illustrated with the pyramid shown in Fig. 14.7.

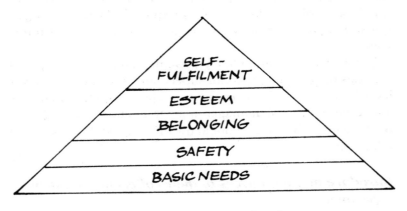

Figure 14.7 Five levels of need

Table 14.1 shows how you can help—or at least not hinder the fulfilment of these needs in your colleagues.

Make personal contact with new colleagues

When new supervisors are appointed, go over and pay them a visit to welcome them into the supervisory team and let them know how you can help.

Table 14.1

Their needs	Points to observe when dealing with colleagues
Self-fulfilment Concern with personal growth, setting challenging standards of self-achievement.	Avoid causing them frustration. Help them to achieve their legitimate goals.
Esteem Seeking opportunities to display competence so as to gain social or professional rewards.	Recognize their contribution. Don't bypass them. Don't 'knock' them.
Belonging Wishing to feel accepted and appreciated by others.	Show a friendly attitude. Inform them. Seek their opinion on matters which touch upon their areas of responsibility.
Safety Need for security, orderliness, risk-avoidance and sense of performance.	Avoid giving them nasty surprises. Don't buck the system they have established for their department.
Basic Survival needs like food, shelter, warmth.	You cannot do much about these except symbolically (a cup of coffee when they visit you?).

Keep your colleagues informed

Always ask yourself 'Who needs to know, who would like to know about this decision we have made, or this new information?' An open attitude about information sharing will encourage them to do the same for you.

Consult them

The decisions you make will often affect colleagues so involve them in your decision making by seeking their opinions and, if necessary, their permission. They can often make constructive and helpful suggestions.

Identify interdepartmental friction points and work out a plan for reducing the heat generated there

A cooperative spirit has to be built up one brick at a time, so tackle friction points systematically by discussing with your colleagues the main problem area and resolving it, then moving on to the next. For example, the problem may be that production operators consider the fitters are too leisurely about moving into action when there is a breakdown and it may be possible to agree that each fitter should have a separate area to patrol, and be judged on the number of hours that the machines are kept running as against breakdown time. Having resolved this, you could perhaps move on to discuss ways of preventing breakdowns through better operator training. The aim must be to take positive cumulative steps to eliminate friction points.

Conclusion

We are living in the age of the Organization Man. This doesn't mean, though, that we all have to be unreasoning cogs in the machine. By understanding the mechanics of organizations you can play your part in keeping yours efficient.

If you can think analytically about your organization (tempering your judgement with tact), the suggestions you put forward and contributions you make as a member of the management team will be wiser and sounder.

Table 14.2 Checklist on interdepartmental liaison

Questions	×✓	Notes
1. Is there evidence of an interchange of ideas between you and other departmental heads?		
2. Is there a smooth flow of work from your department and section and those on either side of it?		
3. Do you consult the specialists in the organization?		
4. Do you know who to go to with your questions or those raised by the staff?		
5. Do you have a clear understanding of the borderline between your responsibilities and others'?		
6. Do you maintain a good working relationship with colleagues?		
7. Do you respect colleagues' time at meetings by being punctual?		

Questions

1. In reviewing the duties of a personnel department it might be claimed that the supervisor's authority is undermined. Comment on this statement.
2. Name five defects in the structure of an organization which could seriously affect the efficiency of supervisors, and explain why.
3. A supervisor should not have too many people to manage. What is likely to happen if this is the case, and what factors will influence the number that can be controlled?
4. Do you consider yourself as part of management? Do other supervisors? Give your reasons.

15. *What you can do to improve work methods*

How efficient are the work methods in your department? You may have a work study department who have as one of their main duties the task of looking at the way in which jobs are done throughout the company and trying to rearrange the tools, workplace, sequence of operations and methods of operating so that less effort will be wasted and more effective work done. But don't leave it all to them.

Unless every supervisor and manager is aware of the basic principles involved in method improvement, the staff may find themselves wasting their energies on useless or inefficient tasks.

Example

Here is an example of one such useless routine which came to light only through an industrial accident. The story began years ago when an operator was instructed to work a valve to blow steam down a pipeline into a catchpot outside. But 27 years previously alternative arrangements had been made and there was no longer any need to operate the valve. No one ever told the operator to stop and he carried on operating the valve until one day it was opened when somebody was walking by the catchpot outside. The pot was full of steam and the passer-by was splashed with water. Only when the accident was investigated were the 27 years of useless work discovered.

It's no use waiting until work study identifies waste. In factories, offices and shops all over the country unproductive jobs are being carried out. Staff are filing away copies of documents that will never be referred to, keeping statistics that were needed five years ago when someone else was chairman but are not wanted by his successor, doing jobs machines could do, and many are doing them unsystematically. It all adds up to an appalling waste of resources and gives staff the impression that nobody cares very much what they do with their time.

How do you analyse jobs of work to find easier ways of doing them? If, as the work study people say, 'There's always a better way', how do you set about finding it?

The following procedure for improving work methods is designed to make better use of manpower, machinery and materials. It doesn't depend on just casually spotting an inefficient part of the process, but on systematically breaking the procedure into steps and challenging whether each step needs to be taken. If it is necessary, it challenges whether the action in question is being performed in the most effective way.

Could the whole job be eliminated?

It is important to ask this question first. The operator who for 27 years worked the steam valve might have tried to find some more ingenious methods of doing it (a lever instead of a tap, a rope attached to the lever, etc.), but would have been wasting time in any case, because the job itself was unnecessary.

Six steps to method improvement

1. *Choose the job*   Take any process carried out in your section which looks as though it could be done more safely, more easily, with less movement, or in such a way that it would eliminate bottlenecks.
2. *Record the sequence of actions involved*   You have to note on paper an accurate breakdown of the steps or stages of the process. Tell your staff what you are trying to do. Consult

them about the job and enlist their support in finding a better way of doing it. They will certainly accept a new method more readily if they have played a part in devising it.

3. *Examine the method* Table 15.1 shows the questions to ask.

4. *Develop the new method* Review all the ideas which your questions have raised. Eliminate as many unnecessary steps as you can, simplify those you cannot eliminate, and make sure the sequence is logical. Ensure that it is safe. Make a chart showing the new method and submit it for your boss's approval if you are satisfied that it is really a significant improvement.

5. *Install the new method* When you have received approval for it, gauge the right time to put it in, e.g., before or after the holidays, New Year, when a particular person retires, perhaps even tomorrow. Convince all concerned and brief them or train them properly on the new procedure.

6. *Maintain it* Check up frequently at first. Is it achieving the expected result? If not, why not—and what must be done to see that it does?

Many supervisors are good at doing their jobs as they are at present but not so many are actively trying to introduce changes for the sake of productivity, safety, or the elimination of bottlenecks. You may find at first that your idea is accepted with only lukewarm enthusiasm, but you must try to sell it if it is a good one, and not be too easily put off.

Other method study tools

Besides the 'questioning technique', as this is called, there are a number of other very useful tools for improving efficiency. These include process charts which give you a simplified picture of the job, bar charts showing labour utilization, string diagrams for measuring distances travelled in the course of the work, and many other ingenious ways of looking at the job and the effort involved. If you have never attended a work study

Table 15.1 Jobs methods—the questioning technique

What is achieved?	Is it necessary? Why?	What other achievement would be better?
Where is it done?	Why there?	What other place would be better?
When is it done?	Why then?	What other time would be better?
Who does it?	Why that person?	What other person would be better?
How is it done?	Why in that way?	What other way would be better?
		Note all ideas

Consider

Safety

Design

Layout

Equipment

Materials

appreciation course of about a week's duration, I would strongly recommend this to you. The equivalent course for office staff is known as 'Organization, Methods, and Information Technology'.

Employee involvement

It is a good idea to involve your staff closely in any method improvement plan for two reasons:

1. They are closest to the work, they know the problems, and usually have many good ideas.
2. Their involvement will enhance the feeling of teamwork and make them more likely to go along with the new method when it has been developed.

Here are some good questions to ask each member of your team:

- What wastes your time?
- What irritates you?
- What could be done differently?
- What need not be done at all?

Quality Circles

The Japanese have developed and widely applied an idea which originated in America, the concept of *Quality Circles*. The results in terms of product reliability and employee involvement have been dramatic.

The idea is to form groups of volunteers from the shop floor whose task is to select any quality problem and bring their ideas, knowledge and experience to bear on it. They spend typically one hour every week in the company's time (and very often a considerable amount of their own leisure time) looking into a particular problem and preparing a presentation to management. The ideal number in a group is from six to ten people.

British companies have not been slow to adopt the idea and some have widened it to look into other aspects besides product quality. The results have been extremely encouraging.

Questions

1. Outline the six steps of method improvement.
2. What is meant by the *questioning technique* in methods planning?
3. What are the advantages of *involving* employees in methods planning, and how would you go about getting them involved?
4. Could Quality Circles be introduced in your company? What benefit would they bring and what obstacles might you have to overcome in getting them accepted?

16. *Cost reduction*

Not all the advice on cost reduction applies to every supervisor, so this chapter is divided into three parts:

Cost reduction for all supervisors   Everything in this section is likely to apply to you whatever kind of work you do.

Supplement for factory production supervisors   Here are some extra ideas which you will find helpful if you work on production in a factory.

Some useful cost accounting terms   These will be of value if you have to work with budgets or are interested in knowing more about cost accounting.

Cost reduction for all supervisors

Budgeting

Companies which do not get their sums right are likely to put themselves rapidly out of business.

A budget is like a route map through the finances of the coming year, predicting the expected income and planned outgoings. If we are talking about businesses, the income is derived from sales of goods and services; if we are thinking of government departments and other organizations which are financed through fixed revenues (such as schools or the fire service, for example) then this income takes the form of regular cash injections from rates, taxes, grants, etc.

As in all other aspects of management there are five main stages in a budget, as shown in Fig. 16.1.

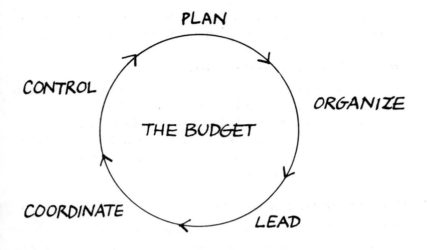

Figure 16.1 Five stages in a budget

1. *The budget has to be planned* What will be the expected income? How do we propose to use it, and when?

2. *It has to be organized* Who is going to prepare it? Answer—everybody in the organization who can make useful predictions—ideally right down to the cleaner deciding whether more plastic bags and disinfectant are required. There must be somebody who collates all this information—usually the accountant.

3. *Those who are going to produce it and work to it must be motivated* This will be achieved if they are consulted and their commitment is obtained.

4. *The budget has to be coordinated* It is no use cutting back production to save costs if the sales department plan to make the biggest ever sales drive.

5. *Finally, it has to be controlled* Month by month and perhaps more frequently every manager who produces income or spends it needs to know if he or she is keeping within the

guidelines laid down, and if not what the variance is (up or down) so that necessary corrections can be made quickly.

What is increased productivity?

If a factory produces 1000 units a day at a cost of £100 000 and an extension is built so that it can produce 2000 for £200 000, its production will double but its productivity will be the same. Productivity is the ratio of input to output and you raise it by getting proportionally more out than you put in. You can only do this by cutting the unit cost of production.

Why cost reduction matters

Any firm which cannot improve its productivity each year is in fact sliding backwards. Your company's product is competing with others making the same thing who are trying to take a greater share of the market. It is also competing with firms making different goods because potential customers have only a limited number of pounds and an unlimited number of wants to satisfy. They will use their money on the things that give best value first, so if you make refrigerators you may be competing with anybody, from the carpet manufacturer to the television company. It won't do to cut prices by paring down dividend payments to shareholders either. In the first place there isn't much payable after tax has been deducted and a sizeable sum has been ploughed back into the business, and moreover nobody will want to invest in the firm next time it needs money to expand. If investors cannot earn more than a building society pays they are unlikely to put their money into industry where there are always risks.

The role of the cost accountant

Cost accountants produce facts and figures so that management can make the best use of materials, staff and machines available. They compare a new method of manufacture with the present one and tell you if you will save money. They produce figures showing how actual expenditure and performance compares with forecasted budgets or standard costs. The figures produced are like the rev. counter, thermometer and speedometer which tell the driver of an engine how it is running. The supervisor is the key person here. It is the supervisor, not the accountant, who can save money.

If there are no proper control figures a company can go seriously off the rails before anyone realizes that anything is wrong. If you are fortunate enough to have access to cost data, make sure that you know how to interpret them. Ask the accountant to explain where your costs are high or out of line. Go through your budgetary returns together and learn how to read your score. *Management is measurement*, and if somebody has given you the measurements it is up to you to learn how to interpret them. Incidentally, the information you receive from the system is only as accurate as the information you feed in, so be sure that you charge expenses to the correct account number.

How does the supervisor influence cost?

You can directly affect:
- how diligently people work;
- the methods they use;
- their skill;
- the time which is lost;
- the extra work which is sometimes done;
- the materials which are wasted.

The chapters 'Achieving results through people', 'Removing frustration', 'What you can do to improve work methods' and 'Your responsibility for training' give guidance on the first three points listed above.

Cutting cost time

Your company's task is to deliver quality products at the time they are wanted and at the right price. If the job comes out in good time, you save on payroll and machine time and so help in the long term to cut prices. Moreover, you help to keep the customers happy and they will want to buy more if the sales department can promise earlier deliveries. Time is often thrown away, but you do not notice this form of waste so much because it doesn't litter the floor. Yet accumulated lost minutes can cost thousands. Wasted time and delay in your department may produce unnecessary expense in others. Here is how an assembly department in a factory could suffer, if previous departments were running late:

- idle time waiting for parts to arrive;
- overtime to make up for lost time to meet delivery dates;
- penalty payments to customers for late deliveries;
- airfreight charges on shortages which could not be shipped with the machines.

Six ideas for improving productivity, whatever you supervise

1. *Half jobs* Sometimes a new responsibility comes along which doesn't really occupy a person for a whole day and yet somebody is assigned to it full-time. It is important to have a look at these half jobs now and again and see if two of them can be combined into one. Perhaps somebody doing a £10 000 a year job spends many hours a month on work which a £5000 a year employee could do. This may not be as wasteful as it looks if by so doing you avoid taking a new person on the payroll with all the necessary overheads.

2. *Make sure the next job is ready* Unless the next job is lined up, staff tend to slacken off their pace and effort to match the work in hand. Make sure that they know the next job is there.

3. *Reduce material costs* Encourage your staff to take care with the small items as well the expensive ones. Nuts, bolts, pencils and paperclips cost very little singly, but multiply them by a few hundred for a number of people

wasting them and another few score for the number of times per year and it soon mounts up. Tell them about this sort of wastage. If you have,to throw away useless materials or tools, let purchasing department know about it, because they may think that they have been getting a bargain. Moreover, they may be able to obtain credit from the suppliers. Perhaps you can also persuade purchasing department to try for a different material, a casting instead of a machined piece, strips instead of sheets, a smaller size perhaps? When the job was set up the present material might have been the best or the only one they could find, but now you can probably do better. Sometimes the product may be made at great cost in the factory when it could be bought more cheaply outside. Try to get costs and figures to support your argument.

In supermarkets great piles of tins or carelessly heaped bars of soaps are used to make the customer feel extravagant. Masses of materials have that psychological effect in the factory too, so counteract it by restoring your staff's cost awareness. Persuade them to try to cut one more piece out of a length, or a sheet or a pound. Don't let them waste the first dozen yards on the start-up, or let the first two gallons of fluid run off before they take what they need. Encourage them to report waste when they see it.

4. *Fatigue costs money*   If you have a work study section ask their advice on how some of the jobs in your department could be made less tiring. Many jobs are harder than they need be because tools and materials are difficult to reach; a chair or bench of the wrong height can cause strain on the back and neck; trays of completed batches may be too big, too small, too heavy or too awkward; excessive time and effort may be used in hunting for tools or gauges. The work study specialist is trained to use a great many methods-study techniques for making jobs easier and faster.

ARE TOOLS AND MATERIALS EASY TO REACH?

5. *A question of teamwork* Cutting costs is like most of management, a question of teamwork. Besides your cost accountant, you can ask for the help of all these service departments:

- engineering;
- stores;
- purchasing;
- methods planning;
- industrial relations;
- quality control;
- production control, etc.

Above all don't overlook the people nearest to the cost leaks—your own team on the shop floor. One supervisor was wondering why Frank Gardner, an assembly worker, was twice as quick as the rest. Then they discovered that Frank had installed hooks on the upright at the back of his bench; all his tools were set out in the order he needed them, and he would reach for the one he wanted without looking up from his work. A suggestion scheme can bring out such ideas as these, create cooperation, and provide staff with a reward for their help.

By consulting them, you will spot wastage that could have been overlooked, you will make them cost conscious, and above all, you will help to create a sense of partnership on the job.

6. *Learn how to do value analysis* Value analysis, which is an extension of the methods planning techniques mentioned later in this book, means studying a product to see whether it can be made more cheaply and still give the required service and performance. Many companies have made great savings with this approach. For example, 77 per cent was cut off the cost of manufacturing a small spring in one firm and in another the cost of pump bases was reduced by two-thirds.

A team consisting of departments such as design, production, purchasing and sales select a bestseller from the range of products or components and then go through the following stages:

(a) *Information stage* Get all the data and information relevant to the product.

(b) *Speculation stage*

- Can the job be done another way and at lower cost?
- Can something else be used instead?
- Can dimensions be reduced?
- Can waste in manufacture be reduced?
- Are correct limits or finishes specified?
- Can standard components be used instead of specials?
- Can we buy out cheaper? Can we make cheaper?
- Can cheaper components be substituted to do the jobs?
- Can alternative material be used?

(c) *'Brainstorming': letting ideas pour out* This stage is carried out as a team discussion to which suppliers may also be invited so that they can make suggestions from their knowledge of their own products. It is important that no one should hold an inquest as to why certain mistakes have not been spotted before, otherwise everyone will become too defensive to cooperate. While the ideas are being offered and listed all present have to guard against their negative reactions such as 'They won't accept it', 'We've tried it', 'Why try it?' and 'What's wrong with our present way?'.

(d) *Investigation stage* The team breaks up and mulls over these ideas for a week or two.

(e) *Recommendation stage* A meeting is held to assess ideas and decide which ones to put to management.

(f) *Implementation stage* Before implementing the ideas which have been adopted, top management consults the unions in order to pave the way for acceptance on the shop floor.

Value analysis is useful because nobody tends to look at products which have been going well for some time. Although the technique is really just organized common sense, the discipline and teamwork of this approach lead to discoveries which individual intelligence would be unlikely to spot. Even if your company does not adopt value analysis in a formal way, you can make use of the basic ideas behind it.

Supplement for factory production supervisors

If you are a production supervisor in a factory, try some of these additional tips.

Machine-paced jobs with slack

Sometimes an operator is only working at half speed because the job is machine-paced and it is running slowly. It is important to check up on machine speeds and see whether they are adjusted to give the best output without overworking the operator.

Machine down-time

There will be less down-time if you develop in an employee a sense that this is his machine, and encourage him to take a pride in it, do minor adjustments and keep it running. Let him know how much it cost to buy new. You can train people to report suspicious machine noises or smells and so avoid serious damage.

AN EMPLOYEE WILL TAKE PRIDE IN HIS MACHINE

If the machine breaks down, tell the operator to:

- Give as much information as possible to maintenance department so that the fitter can come prepared.
- Show or describe to the fitter the last piece off the machine.
- Explain the symptoms.
- Say whether it has happened before.

If the operator caused the accident he or she should be encouraged to admit how it happened so that the fault can quickly be located. If a machine frequently goes out of action, talk to your maintenance department about why it is costing you so much. It may pay to keep a record of how often it is down. Preventive maintenance could also be the answer. Perhaps it would even pay to have a new machine. The maintenance engineer doesn't always know how much it is costing you, and you may have to produce some figures to prove your case.

Make sure that staff report waiting time

Some departments have workcards which show waiting time. If yours has, are you sure that your staff record all their downtime and don't hide it because they think it may cause you trouble? It helps if waiting time can be recorded in categories:

- wait for work;
- wait for materials;
- wait for supervisor;
- wait for inspector;
- wait for fork lift truck, etc.

Many supervisors spend 15 minutes a day looking through the workcards in their department. By doing this you can find out about any delays or holdups before these returns leave the department and arrive on the desk of somebody else who might ask awkward questions.

If an incentive scheme is operating in your department, insist that claims for waiting time are put in immediately. If you get an omnibus claim at the end of the week, you cannot remember all the details and in any case it is too late for any remedies.

Cut down on unnecessary work

One form of extra work results from wasted set-up time when a rush job comes along and just has to go through on a particular machine which is all set for production, or which is going flat out, but you have to break the run. There is not much you can do about this except perhaps to persuade your boss to allow you to make up, in slack time, some of the most often-used spares.

Sometimes you can persuade production control to allow you to combine production orders which are similar. Perhaps the greatest hidden cost is in what happens to people's attitude to the work . . . 'Why bother to break our necks on this job? . . . we shall have to undo all our work again.' 'Why should we bother to try and save a few pennies in time? . . . those people up in the office are throwing away hundreds of pounds.' 'This outfit is a shambles, the left hand doesn't know what the right hand is doing.'

It is vital to combat this feeling. You will have delivery and priority problems every day that your firm has customers, so recognize that these are the circumstances you have to work under and help the team to adopt the right attitude towards them. Try to streamline methods of changeover. Re-arrange your set-up sequences. Sometimes the answer is in training a more versatile crew. It may be worth recording set-up time so that the cost of excessive changes can be accurately measured against the benefits.

Rework

Scrap means wasted material and time spent doing the job again. Check whether the trouble is with the tools. Are people's implements blunt or inaccurate? Are their measuring or recording instruments in need of adjustment? Get the toolroom to routine-check tools before issue. Find out from the toolroom who is misusing them and, without making any one feel that they are being picked on, give some tips on tool care.

If you have repeated defects of a similar kind, track down the cause. Get back to those who are producing scrap and set them on the right lines. Encourage operators not to hide known rejects among a trayful of good parts. Train them to detect a trend towards spoilage (e.g. punch holes deteriorating with each press movement) and take action before the first reject is produced rather than after. Scrap should be declared at once, otherwise further operations may be wasted later and time lost if replacements have to be ordered.

Standards of finish

The security officer wanted a piece of wood to place under the back of the key cabinet to stop it from rocking on the uneven floor boards. She asked the carpenter's shop for a block $\frac{1}{2}'' \times 2'' \times 6''$. In came a piece of oak four days later, sanded and varnished, neat enough to serve as the works director's paperweight. It sounds fantastic, but failure to specify standards often means you receive something which is too good or not good enough. You may need to ask for some proper standards —perhaps even a set of samples if you often have doubt about the type of finish needed.

Useful cost accounting terms to know

Companies vary in their attention to budgetary control and standard costing. Some supervisors never see a budget at all, but companies increasingly feel it is important to provide cost information to all managers and supervisors and encourage front line supervision to interpret and act on it.

If you don't fully understand what these computer printouts mean or how you can use them, ask the cost accountant or your department head to go over them with you.

The following are some useful accounting terms—read them up and then check your understanding of them by answering the quiz at the end of the chapter.

Labour costs

The direct labour cost—the gross wages paid to staff who work directly on the product, e.g. grinder, lathe operator, extrusion press operators, etc.

The indirect labour cost—the office staff, supervisor and floor-sweeper are necessary to production but their work is contributory rather than direct. Their wages and salaries are called 'indirect labour costs'.

Material costs

The direct material cost is the value of the materials which go into the product. They include, for example, the plastic, steel and rubber in your car.

The indirect material costs are the costs of such things as grinding wheels and lubricants. You could not do without them but they never form part of the finished article.

Sometimes there are borderline cases which might be classed as 'direct' or 'indirect', whether under the heading of labour or material. Your cost accountant will give a ruling if asked.

Overhead costs

These are all the indirect labour and indirect material costs from your department and others, plus managers' salaries, the cost accountant and all the service departments. Rent and rates come into this category and so do all your firm's expenses which cannot be classified as direct materials or labour.

Variable indirect overheads

These are items which vary sharply in proportion to the amount of throughput and include oil and lubricants, cutting tools and machine fuel; and on the labour side, the wages of truck and crane drivers, labourers and sweepers.

Fixed indirect overheads

These do not vary much whatever the throughput and include, on the material side for example, replacement lamps for factory lighting; and on the wages side, such things as the wages of the security guard or telephone switchboard operator. Rent, rates and depreciation are also classed as fixed overheads.

Standard costing procedure

This amounts to budgeting the cost per item or number of items under 'normal' conditions. Once standard costs are fixed, you can compare them with the money spent as the job progresses. If you find that you are over-spending you can find out why and then decide what to do about it. Standard costing also enables the firm to predict accurately what the product will cost and so give the customer more competitive, but safer, estimates.

Break even (recovery of overheads)

If a television factory were to produce only one set a day, the cost of production would include, besides the direct costs, the whole of that day's overheads and indirect labour and materials —over £20 000. The break even point for recovery of overheads and indirect costs is reached when enough sets are produced to share the overheads and, when direct costs are added, make neither a loss nor a profit.

Table 16.1 shows an example of a television factory where the variable cost may be £300 per set (direct wages, direct materials and variable overheads) and the fixed expenses £20 000 per day with a selling price (ex factory) of £500.

Table 16.1 **Analysing break even point**

Output per day (sets)	90	100	110	120
	£	£	£	£
Variable cost £300 each	27 000	30 000	33 000	36 000
Fixed cost	20 000	20 000	20 000	20 000
Total cost	47 000	50 000	53 000	56 000
Selling price at £500 each	45 000	50 000	55 000	60 000
Loss per day	2000	—	—	—
Profit	—	—	2000	4000

The break even point is 100 sets per day since, at that output, the sales value equals the total cost. If the output falls to 90 sets per day, there is a loss due to unrecovered fixed overheads. If it rises above 100 a profit is made and it increases steadily from then onwards.

Figure 16.2 shows how it looks in the form of a graph.

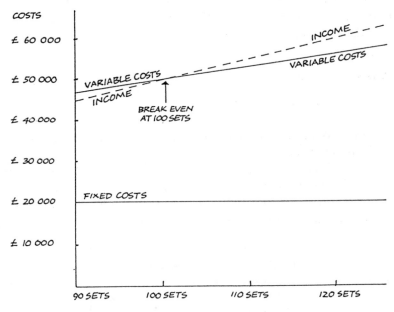

Note: Your costs are higher than your income for up to 100 sets but if you produce and sell more than 100 you are in profit.

Figure 16.2 Television sets produced and sold

Quiz in cost terms

1. How would you classify the cost of cloth in a tailoring factory?
2. How would you classify the wages of a fork-lift truck driver in your department?
3. 'The break even point (recovery of overheads) is reached when the overheads divided by the units produced equals the selling price.' Is this true or false?

4. Would you classify as a direct or indirect labour cost the wage of a maintenance electrician?
5. What is the term used for overhead costs:
   (a) which rise with the number of units produced?
   (b) which remain fairly static however many are produced?
6. Standard costing predicts the cost of each item or batch. Is this statement true or false?

Answers to quiz

1. Direct material cost.
2. Indirect labour cost.
3. False. What about the direct material and direct wages?
4. Indirect labour.
5. (a) variable overheads;
   (b) fixed overheads.
6. True, provided that the variances from budgeted standard cost are taken into account, e.g., wage awards, etc.

Table 16.2 Checklist on cost consciousness

Questions	✗ ✓	Notes
1. Do the staff work diligently?		
2. Do you ensure good timekeeping and are you yourself a good timekeeper?		
3. Do you make sure that there is full usage of equipment and staff?		
4. Do you keep overtime to the minimum necessary?		
5. Do you have the right number of people, not too few, nor too many?		
6. Do you try to ensure that there are no 'half jobs'?		
7. Do you seek to change any methods which are unduly time wasting?		

Questions	×✓	Notes
8. Do you seek to change any methods which are unduly tiring?		
9. Are the staff properly trained?		
10. Do they show cost consciousness?		
11. Do you ensure that they are not left short of materials, equipment, etc.?		
12. Is little time wasted through equipment being out of action?		
13. Do your staff always report delays and interruptions to the work flow?		
14. Do you check on it to try to remove the causes?		
15. Are you as careful about company STD costs as you would be on your telephone at home?		
16. Do you know the cost of the equipment and materials which your department uses?		
17. Is serious pilfering eliminated?		
18. Does bad equipment cause scrap?		
19. Do you track down and put right recurrent causes of scrap?		
20. Are you putting too much effort into achieving perfection on jobs which do not demand it?		
21. Are standards high enough where they should be?		
22. Could you cut wasted work by achieving better liaison with other departments?		
23. Do people tend to disregard small but frequent wastage in your department?		
24. Are you careful to see that lights, heaters, machinery, etc., are not left on unnecessarily?		

Table 16.2 (*continued*)

Questions	✗ ✓	Notes
25. Do you try to save the company money by talking to the purchasing officer about quality standards or materials?		
26. Is there any evidence of the extravagance resulting from 'seeing plenty around'?		
27. Do you plan staff holidays in order to achieve minimum use of expensive temporary staff from agencies?		
28. What other help could you obtain from the following departments in reducing costs: ● the department for which you provide a service ● accounts ● stores ● purchasing ● organization and methods ● personnel?		
29. Do you ask your staff for their ideas on cutting costs?		
30. Have you a working knowledge of the main principles of work study/methods planning?		

Questions

1. What is standard costing?
2. What are the aims of a cost system in a production unit? What information about costs is of value to the supervisor?
3. Explain what is meant by budgetary control and show the part which a supervisor can be expected to play in the operation of such a system.
4. Outline the ways in which waste can arise in the use of materials and show the main ways in which this waste could be reduced to a minimum.
5. Describe the steps which could be taken to improve productivity in your department.
6. What is meant by the break even point?

17. *Planning and managing your time*

Are you a tram, bus, or taxi?

Time is your most valuable asset and you probably have more freedom than you think when it comes to deciding how to use it, but it does depend on whether your job makes you a tram, bus, or taxi.

Trams have to run on laid down lines. They can only go where the track takes them, and the driver cannot switch the points. Somebody else does that. The only freedom is to start, vary the speed, or stop. Examples of tram jobs are: production-line track operators, postmen, and astronauts, doing what mission control says they must do (for tram jobs need not be menial ones).

Buses have some freedom about where they drive on the road, so long as they follow the route. They may follow diversion signs as long as they cover the specified bus stops and reach the terminus. Examples of bus jobs are: shop assistants, bank managers and waiters.

Taxis can go by whatever route they like to reach their destination, and so have the greatest measure of freedom. Examples of taxi jobs are: sales managers, personnel officers and the self-employed.

Which of these three are you? Trams cannot do very much about time management (except we hope domestically) but most supervisors are either buses, taxis, or somewhere between, so we will assume your job is at this end of the spectrum.

Every day planning

Key results areas

The secret of good time management is to concentrate your efforts in those areas of your job where you can make the greatest impact on productivity, people and resources. In your position you will probably have about six of these key results areas (KRAs for short), and Fig. 17.1 overleaf is an example of what they would look like in a production environment. Adapt it to suit your job.

Pick out and pursue your priority goals in these areas and your effectiveness will soar. In the nineteenth century, the Italian economist and sociologist Vilfredo Pareto observed that '20 per cent of your activities will give you 80 per cent of your results'. The reverse, he commented, was also true. The remaining 80 per cent of your effort will contribute a meagre 20 per cent return. While there may be good reasons for not abandoning altogether the low-yield activities, the greatest effort and attention should go into the high-yield ones.

The need to make time for planning

When you are planning you are not actually producing but preparing to produce. It is tempting to say this is time-wasting and dive straight in, thinking that it is better to press on rather than to sit and consider. Those who do this often get fair results just because they are boiling over with energy and they certainly look busier, but they are not always working as effectively as they might.

People who don't plan waste *manpower* because people are left idle; they waste *materials* because ordering is haphazard and hasty work on materials which have arrived late leads to spoilage; they waste *machine time* because the equipment is not used to the full; and they waste *space* because incoming or outgoing work in progress piles up. Poor planning is also harmful to morale because nobody likes to do unnecesary work as a result of a time-wasting, ill-thought-out system.

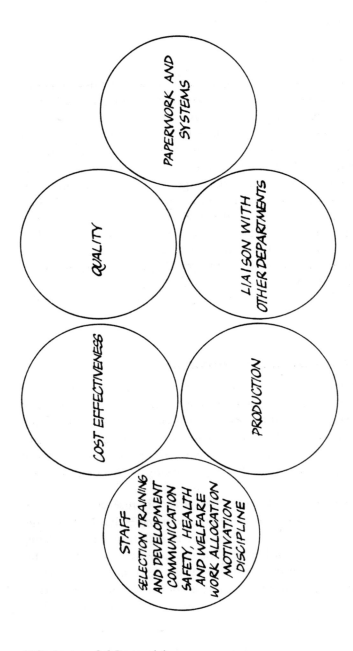

Figure 17.1 Key results areas

QUALITY

PAPERWORK AND SYSTEMS

LIAISON WITH OTHER DEPARTMENTS

COST EFFECTIVENESS

PRODUCTION

STAFF
SELECTION TRAINING
AND DEVELOPMENT
COMMUNICATION
SAFETY, HEALTH
AND WELFARE
WORK ALLOCATION
MOTIVATION
DISCIPLINE

We can't do much to reduce the amount of work we have to get through, but we can master it by organizing it, establishing priorities, delegating and tackling things systematically. You may consider that with a full head of steam you can go through your workload without planning, but how promotable are you on that basis? Your superiors may be looking for people whose attributes in their present jobs fit them for the next one up, so use *forethought* as well as sheer drive.

Organizing your desk

The volume of paperwork, memos, computer printouts and suppliers' brochures increases every month, so a well organized desk is essential. One supervisor says that until last week she hadn't realized that her desk had a wooden top!

Five years ago the average production supervisor's filing system consisted of a pile of papers held down by a cog wheel with a tooth missing. Today you do need a reasonable desk with paperwork trays and some drawers for your folders. A filing cabinet may be an essential item, too, because it doesn't inspire much confidence if people can come into your office and see confidential memos lying about. Figure 17.2 shows a suggested desk layout. Adjust it to suit your needs and the space and furniture you have available.

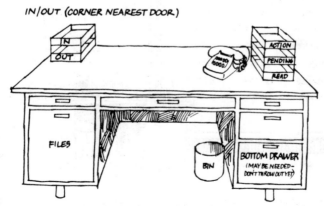

Figure 17.2 **Suggested desk layout**

Draw up a schedule of pending jobs

The best organized managers and supervisors prepare the night before a list of jobs for the following day. Write down everything you wish to accomplish during the day, including both the *reactive* jobs—such as dealing with a request, complaint, or instruction—and the *creative* jobs in your key results areas—the ones which are going to help expand the business or improve the way things run (such as initiating a better system or opening up new opportunities).

Then allocate priorities—but not only on the basis of how *urgent* a matter is. You must also take into account how *important* it is.

KEEP A LIST OF PENDING JOBS

Urgent or important

Your job may be by its very nature the kind in which urgent matters arise frequently. In all supervisory positions you need to establish procedures and contingency arrangements for frequently occurring urgent jobs; work steadily towards fire prevention so that you are less frequently fire-fighting. Unless you do this you may find yourself dealing with emergencies all day long and not getting the real job done at all.

It is vital to be able to distinguish between those things which are *urgent* and those which are *important*. For example, it may be urgent to fill up your fuel tank before the petrol price increases at midnight, but it is not important. On the other hand a very important matter may not be urgent. For example, a son or daughter might be underachieving at school, but this usually does not require action within 48 hours. The danger occurs when we fail to schedule important actions and are busily doing the urgent but trivial jobs. If something is both urgent *and* important then of course it goes to the top of the priority list.

How would you classify the following? Note down U—urgent; I—important; or U/I—urgent and important. The answers are given at the end of the chapter.

1. Cashing in your book of trading stamps before the offer closes tomorrow.
2. Noting your car key number in your diary.
3. Renewing your RAC/AA membership which expires tomorrow.
4. Calling in specialists to deal with woodworm in the attic.
5. Replacing the used fire extinguisher in the paint shop.
6. Doing something about the persistent bad workmanship and poor timekeeping of an employee who has been with your company 11 years and has not responded to numerous warnings.
7. Counselling the long-service employee who has slipped into a rut and is adopting a lackadaisical attitude.

8. Getting the worn flex changed on the department's only electric drill which is in frequent use.
9. Catching the post with your football coupon.
10. Getting to your car before the traffic warden does.

Some important projects are long-term ones which will take months if not years to complete. In this category are: designing a new machine, extending the premises, computerizing your systems, or taking an exam for a professional qualification. The approach to use here is what Alan Lakein calls the 'Swiss cheese' technique. You work away at it one hole at a time, until eventually it is completed.

If you don't start by making the first hole, you will never complete the job, so you have to break the project down into short tasks and set about tackling them. It is very tempting to say 'I needn't revise for the exam until a week before, then I'll shut myself away for seven days with an icebag on my head.' Unfortunately the long unbroken period of time never seems to materialize. It is better to spend an hour or two each night and two half-days every weekend during the two months run up to the exam, if you want to have a clear head on the day.

So next time it is 12.20 and you want to use the ten minutes before lunch to the best advantage, drill a hole in your Swiss cheese. *Important* beats *urgent*! The form shown in Fig. 17.3 illustrates a simple day-plan format on which you can list work, non-work (domestic) and long-term (Swiss cheese) duties.

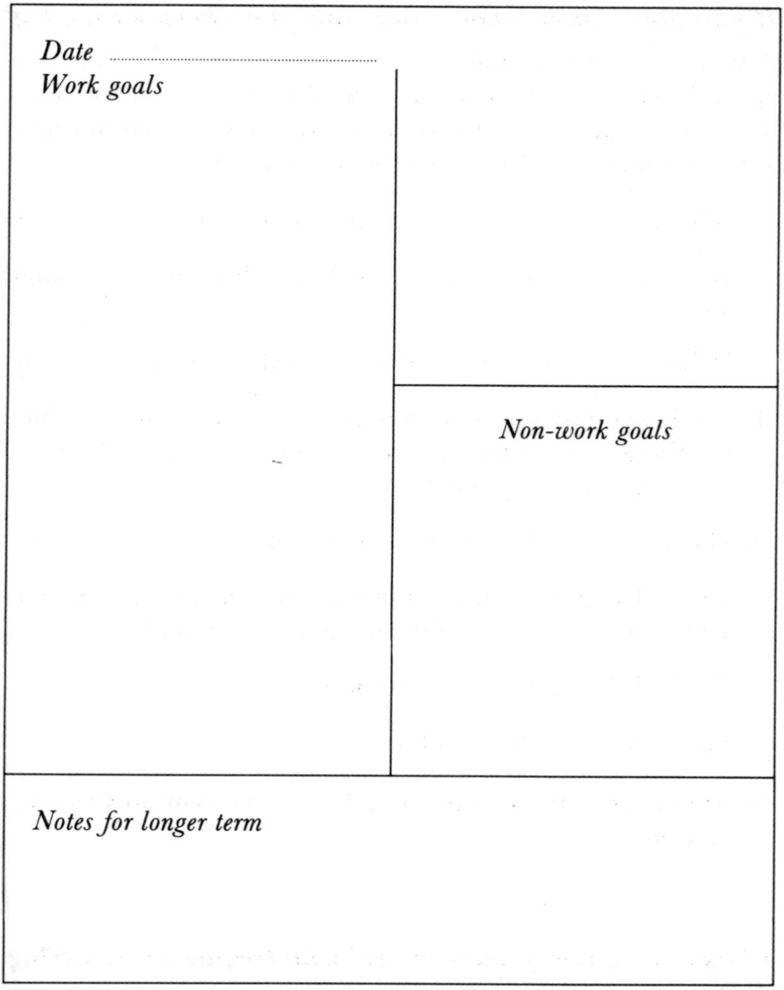

Date ....

Work goals

Non-work goals

Notes for longer term

Fig. 17.3   Daily goal planning sheet

If you don't know where your time goes, keep a time log

A very good way of stopping time wastage is to log how you spend it. For three days you keep track of everything you do—dividing the day up into half-hour slots. Then you examine how you spent that time by asking the following questions:

1. What did I notice as I was doing my time log?

2. What areas/subjects/items am I spending too much time on?

3. What areas/subjects/items am I spending too little time on?

4. Am I devoting time to work which really does not contribute anything and can therefore be cut out altogether? (Does my time log match my KRAs)?

5. Could some tasks be delegated to others?

6. Could I regroup some of the work so that I do not have to change so frequently from one task to another?

7. Could I devote set times to specific tasks?

8. Can some work be simplified?

9. What two or three steps could I now take to improve my use of time?

Work out simple systems to deal with frequently recurring jobs

Instead of having to think out the sequence of events to be followed in the case of—say—a power failure, or a shutdown for preventive maintenance, work out the best system for dealing with a contingency and train your people to use it. In this way you will be able to delegate more. Perhaps a precedent exists and somebody has already done this job before, so check to see.

Example

In the production department of one of the Shell oil fields in Venezuela an ingenious system was devised to shorten the time it took to replace the drive belts which worked the well-head pumps. Operators used to have to go to the particular well whose drive belt had worn and snapped, measure the length (they were non-standard) required, return to base and have a belt of that size cut, then drive to the well again and fit the belt. This system was changed by the supervisor in charge who made a list of all the wells and a note of the belt size required for each. Now when there is a breakage the operator looks up the well number, checks the belt size, makes one up, and goes out to fit it, thus making only one journey instead of two.

Consider using a year-to-view work organizer

These are wall charts, about three feet across by two feet high, divided into months and days showing the whole year. They are excellent for programming activities over long periods, showing public holidays and people's vacations, giving you an overall view of your commitments so that you can see when your peak periods of activity occur and when you will be free to undertake special assignments. They are also useful for reviewing past activities if you are ever asked for that sort of information.

Use checklists

Sales representatives who have to make frequent trips away from home don't leave it to memory every time they pack a case. In the wardrobe there is a checklist of every item that must go in. Packing is a simple job—they just check off shirts, underclothes, toothbrushes, etc., and make sure that nothing is forgotten.

Perhaps checklists could save you a lot of mental effort. They can be used for lists of tools and materials for special jobs, safety inspections, etc., and make job delegation that much easier.

Checklists can remind you of those periodic jobs. Table 17.1 shows an example of how one supervisor drew up an inspection schedule and earned the reputation of never missing a trick.

Larks and owls

Tackle tough jobs when you are at your best, and this does not necessarily mean first thing in the morning. Everyone is a *lark* or an *owl* to a greater or lesser extent. If you accept whichever you are and schedule your day accordingly, you will accomplish more.

Larks come in full of bounce and ready to face the day, able to tackle the hardest job with gusto. *Owls* at this time are still struggling to get their eyes open and have to fortify themselves with a cup of coffee before they can tackle the day's work at all.

If you are an owl, save your most demanding jobs for later in the day and use the early morning to get routine stuff out of the way. Owls are still going strong later on when the larks are worn out.

Planning the big job

The schedule of pending items is a good method of deciding priorities when you have a large number of small jobs to do, but how do you go about planning a big project like organizing— say—the move of your department's equipment and machinery to a new location? The four steps outlined below should help you with major projects.

Define the objective

In this case it would be 'to move all the machinery from department A to department B and have it operational in 24 hours from Saturday at noon'.

Do a job breakdown

Divide your paper vertically down the middle with a line and write in the left-hand column all the things you can think of which you will have to consider about the move. Don't worry about the order, just write them down as they come into your mind, as shown in Table 17.2 on page 212.

Table 17.1 Inspection schedule

Item	1/4	8/4	17/4	10/5	20/5	12/6	14/6	26/6	17/7	Why is this item being followed up so much? / Why is this item being neglected?
Hand tools	1/4								17/7	Why is this item being followed up so much?
First aid pack	2/4									Why is this item being neglected?
Gangways	3/4	4/5	13/5	21/6						
Bench tops	3/4	6/5	10/6	19/6						
Air lines	2/4	7/5	13/6							
Belt drives	3/4	7/5	10/6	19/6						
Spares kit	3/4	14/4	28/5	21/5		*Smith weak – see him*				
Fire extinguisher	4/4	9/5	10/6	27/6						Pencilled note to be erased when actioned
Emer. exits	2/4	8/5	14/6		*no follow-up needed for one month*					
Prod. tickets	4/4	29/4	10/5	27/6						Spaces left for insertion of new items
Toilets	4/4	10/5	21/6							

Date checked (column group heading)

Produced by kind permission of the Industrial Society Inc.

Table 17.2

Item	Detail
Transport Position of machines Manpower for move Power (disconnecting and connecting) Fitters	

When you have thought of as many items as you can, pick out the one which others depend on and start your detailed planning of that. Then begin asking the questions: what, why, how, where, when. They are like a set of spanners, because you use them when they fit. In this case 'position of machines' comes first. Question *why?* doesn't apply. Question *who?*—who can advise me about the new layout? Answer—check with engineering department. Questions *what, when, how, where* do not apply, so leave them out and go on to the next point.

Now the job breakdown sheet looks like Table 17.3:

Table 17.3

Item	Detail
Transport Position of machines Manpower for move Power (disconnecting and connecting) Fitters	
1. Positioning of machines	Check with engineering department

The next point could be *transport*. Question *why*? doesn't need asking. Question *who*?—who can help with transport? Answer—transportation department. *What*?—what is needed? Answer—1 Mack truck with winch, 1 fork lift. *When*?—when do we want them? Answer—fork-lift truck at Saturday noon shutdown; Mack truck at 2pm (2 hours after shutdown to allow time for fitters to disconnect and unbolt No. 1 machine).

At this point you may remember the need for a lunch break so you put that on your list of items.

Go back to using the 'spanners' on the transport question. There is one more to ask, *where*?—where are the trucks to report? Answer—outside A machine shop. Now the chart looks like Table 17.4

Table 17.4

Item	*Detail*
Transport	
Positioning of machines	
Manpower for move	
Power (disconnecting and connecting)	
Fitters	
Lunch break	
1. Position of machines	Check with engineering department
2. Transport	Consult transportation department
	1 fork-lift truck noon Sat.
	1 Mack truck 2 pm Sat.
	To report outside A machine shop

Now the next question—*manpower*.

Question *why*? doesn't need asking. *Who*?—who should supply labour? Answer—maintenance department for fitters, electrical department for power arrangements, transportation department for labour gang (probably six men) and drivers. *When?*—electrician to have a preliminary look today. Fitters needed on Saturday at noon, labour gang needed at 2pm. *Where?*—A shop. Questions *How?* and *What?* don't need asking.

The planning sheet has gone a stage further (see Table 17.5).

Table 17.5

Item	*Detail*
Labour	Two fitters—maintenance department; required 12 noon Saturday.
	Electrician—electrical department; required Monday 4pm and 12 noon Saturday.
	Six labourers—transportation department; required 2pm Saturday.
	All report to A shop.

. . . and so it goes on through all the remaining questions.

Inform and consult all concerned

Check with the heads of departments on whose services you will have to rely. This includes engineers, maintenance, electrical and personnel department (for overtime authorization). Tell them your plan and ask for their help and suggestions. See them personally. Where appropriate let them have notes in writing.

Follow up

After your plan has been carried out, ask yourself what, if anything, went wrong and learn from your mistakes. Take prompt action to remedy whatever it was that did not go according to plan.

Ensuring your timing is right

The army teaches its officers and NCOs to use the 'D-day minus' principle. When there is a sequence of events which must take place before the job itself begins, work back in time fixing the deadline for each preparatory stage. Suppose your department has to produce a sample of its work for an exhibition staged in London on Friday, 28 May. 28 May is D-day so the assembly and erecting on site of your part of the exhibition must be completed by D-day minus two in order to allow a safety margin.

All components must be transported a day before that— D-day minus three.

Manufacture and inspection must be completed on D-day minus four. And so you carry on until finally you arrive at the date for starting. Don't forget to keep everybody informed— sometimes it is worth giving them a plan along these lines:

20 May—making of components completed.
23　"　—assembly completed.
25　"　—transport to London.
26　"　—erecting on site completed.
27　"　—marketing manager inspects stand.
28　"　—exhibition opens.

If you often have to plan large one-off jobs, use the Critical Path technique

Critical Path (network analysis and PERT are variants) is an aid to the planning, coordination and control of major jobs. You draw a diagram showing the critical path for the project, that is, the sequence of operations which must wait upon each other. If you add up the time each takes you can estimate the earliest completion date.

For example, in decorating a room you have to paint the woodwork before you paper the walls. If the painting takes a day, drying takes a day, and papering takes two days, the total time for the project is four days. If the ceiling needs a coat of emulsion this job can be done at the same time as the woodwork so that it will not lengthen the critical path. But if the householder is fussy and wants the woodwork sanding before the paint is applied, he obviously cannot have this done at the same time as the painting or papering, so it will lengthen the critical path (see Fig. 17.4) unless you take other steps.

With a more complicated project things are less obvious than this, so the diagram is essential. It helps you to see your priorities more clearly, as any delay on the critical path must receive immediate attention. If there should be a delay on one of these jobs, the diagram helps you to spot the implications of it and accurately revise your completion date. Suppose the householder insists on the sanding of the woodwork and yet still requires the job to be ready in four days, you could save a day by using quick drying paint at the following stage.

Figure 17.4 Example of critical path technique

Develop the right habits

The morning inspection

Many supervisors and managers find it a useful timesaver to go round their department once a day to keep in touch. Inspections will prevent you from overlooking things which you would not remember if you did not see. They will make you available for solving problems or answering questions, enable you to check on the progress of newcomers to your department, and provide a fixed opportunity for people to see you so that they are not always interrupting at odd times during the day.

Cultivate the delegating habit

Think who could do the job for you. Chapter 12 gives advice on this.

Tell people who need to be informed

When you receive instructions or think up a plan, remember to ask yourself 'Who must I tell about this?'

Make notes

It is wise to make a regular habit of noting points for action, always in the same spot to avoid hunting around for the particular back of an envelope where it was jotted down for convenience. Some people use a pad of tear-off slips with a carbon paper inserted so that they can give people written instructions and keep a note for reference.

Put things in the same place

Many supervisors who as craftsmen were meticulous about how they put their tools back in their kit box, do not carry their good habits into the office, where they are just as necessary.

Before leaving the subject of planning I should like to mention an incident which happened at the Industrial Society a few years ago. Mrs Byers in the print room would always do a job for you 'yesterday' if you really wanted it, but the workload was impossible even for her on this particular day. 'Laura, I wonder if you could print me a hundred copies of these notes by tomorrow?' She said nothing but looked over her glasses at the door. The way out? No! There was a little note there:

(We cannot find out who wrote this, but it is too good to leave out of this book so, with acknowledgements to the author, here it is):

I belong to no age for men have always hurried.
I prod all human endeavour.
Men believe me necessary—but falsely.
I rushed today because I was not planned yesterday.
I demand excessive energy and concentration.
I override obstacles, but at great expense.
I illustrate the old saying 'haste maketh waste'.
My path is strewn with the evils of overtime,
  mistakes and disappointments.
Accuracy and quality give place to speed.
Ruthlessly I rush on.
I am a rush job.

I AM A RUSH JOB!

Table 17.6 Checklist on planning and managing time

Questions	×√	Notes
1. Do jobs come out to time and of the right standard?		
2. Does the work run smoothly?		
3. Are you able to predict fluctuations?		
4. What plans have you for making the best use of your labour at off-peak times?		
5. Is there evidence of your planning?		
6. Do you distribute work in the most effective way?		
7. Do you decide priorities correctly within your authority?		
8. Do you delegate as far as possible?		
9. Do you make the best use of service departments?		
10. Do you get materials on hand before time?		
11. Does your department cooperate effectively in the team as a whole?		
12. Thinking back over any recent wastage of manpower, materials, machine time or floor space in your department, could you have planned to avoid it?		
13. Do you waste time looking for documents, tools, equipment, etc.?		
14. Are you keeping unnecessary records?		
15. Do you make time for special creative work?		
16. How many of your tasks are rush jobs?		
17. Do you distinguish between urgent and important jobs?		
18. Is there sufficient equipment or a time loss during sharing and waiting?		
19. Is the equipment accessible and properly maintained?		

Table 17.6 (*continued*)

Questions	✕ ✓	Notes
20. Does the layout result in unnecessary movement?		
21. Does it lead to excessive personal conversations and interruptions?		
22. Are the staff seated in the best position in relation to each other and the supervisor?		
23. Do you periodically (every 6 months?) review your departmental layout showing positions of staff, records and equipment?		
24. Have you a good follow-up system?		
25. Do you keep a log book recording the department's activities and messages in and out?		
26. *Backlog* (a) Are the arrears resulting in poor service?		
(b) Are they causing additional work, reminders, issue of additional documents, difficulty in finding papers, failure to put through accounting entries or to advise account amendments in time?		
(c) Are the arrears spread generally or confined to one or a few individuals?		
(d) How did the backlog arise—staff shortages or changes, uneven allocation of work, lack of instruction or help?		
(e) What can be done about it—remove it entirely from the individual, stop allocating further work, redistribute, provide assistance, or have a team blitz?		

Questions	×✓	Notes
(f) What longer-term remedies are necessary to prevent a recurrence? (g) Do you frequently examine the records of work outstanding? 27. Does your diary system never let you down?		

Answers to urgent/important quiz

(NB   These answers apply to *busy* supervisors)
1. Urgent but not important.
2. Important but not urgent.
3. Important but not urgent (unless you are about to undertake a long journey or your car is on the point of collapse).
4. Important, but not urgent; 48 hours won't make any difference.
5. Urgent and important.
6. Important but not urgent.
7. Important but not urgent.
8. Important and urgent.
9. Urgent but not important.
10. Urgent but not important (compared with some matters).

Questions

1. Why is it essential to distinguish between matters which are urgent and those which are important?

2. What are time logs and why are they useful?
3. Describe how you would set about planning a major painting and decorating project in a medium-sized factory which has a two-week summer shutdown.

18. *Using initiative when work is delegated to you*

As a supervisor you have to receive delegated work and think through the problems which arise in the course of your duties. Sometimes the issues involved are not ones on which you are authorized to act, but your boss will want your recommendations.

Completed staffwork

The concept of *completed staffwork* is useful here. This is the study of a problem and the presentation of a solution by a supervisor to a manager in such a way that all that remains to be done by the manager is to give a decision. The more difficult a problem is, the more tendency there is to refer it to the manager in a piecemeal fashion.

It is your job to work out the details, consulting other supervisors and specialists such as personnel, training, industrial engineering staff and, if permissible, appropriate sources of information outside the company.

The impulse which sometimes comes to the supervisor to ask a manager what action to take happens more often when the issue is difficult. It is sometimes accompanied by a feeling of frustration, because it is so easy to ask the manager what to do and it appears easy for the latter to answer. You will be more helpful if you can advise on what you think should happen rather than asking what move you should make. It will alleviate the manager's workload if you can consider alternative solutions and possible courses of action and select what you consider to be the best solution.

HE NEEDS ANSWERS, NOT QUESTIONS

Do not worry your boss with long explanations and memos. Writing a memo to the boss is less useful than writing a memo that can be sent to someone else. Your views should be put in a finished form so that your boss can simply sign it if in agreement. If comment or explanation is required, it will be asked for. The concept of completed staffwork does not preclude a rough draft, but this must not consist of half-baked ideas used as an excuse for shifting the burden to the manager.

This way of operating may result in more work for the supervisor but it gives managers more freedom by shielding them from unnecessary detail. Moreover the supervisor who has a real idea to sell is more likely to achieve its acceptance.

When you have finished your completed staffwork the final test is this:

If you were the manager would you be willing to sign for the solution you have recommended, and stake your professional reputation on it? If not, it's 'back to the drawing board'.

If you adopt this way of working, discussion of the assignment with a manager has a proper place when establishing guidelines and methods of approach. This is particularly advisable in lengthy investigations where, if the terms of reference were not agreed with the manager initially, time could be wasted. Sometimes a progress report is desirable, and you should find out whether your boss needs one. The overriding principle is that you should not dodge the responsibility for thinking a problem through in all its aspects.

Next time you hit a snag with a major project, but have some good ideas about solving it; or you have an idea for improving efficiency, cutting costs or reducing accidents; or your boss has asked you to look into a problem and come up with some recommendations—this could be your cue for some completed staffwork.

If you are in doubt about how your boss would take to this way of working, why not discuss this chapter together?

Preventive and contingency plans

The legend of the sword of Damocles tells how a sword was suspended by a hair over the Greek hero's head. At any time the hair might break. Preventive and contingency plans are arrangements which will either remove the threat (why did he have to just stand there?) or minimize the consequences if the threat should materialize (safety helmet). Good maintenance *prevents* a car breaking down, and a tool kit in the boot is useful for contingency purposes.

You not only keep a minimum stock level of frequently used parts, but you have the telephone number of a supplier who would send them on the panic wagon if the need arose. Always foresee snags and take precautions, besides earning the reputation of having a card or two up your sleeve if the worst comes to the worst.

Creative thinking

Creative thinking is the process of generating ideas, whether these are needed in order to overcome snags or to break new ground. One of the best books on this subject is *Lateral Thinking for Management* by Edward de Bono (McGraw-Hill). He points out that we tend to get into a mental rut and think along tramlines instead of jumping out (laterally) and exploring a wider range of ideas. His ideas for doing this are extremely effective. Without going into the many techniques which he outlines, I should just like to list here a number of thought-provoking questions which you might ask next time you are faced with a difficult problem and you are stumped for ideas. The list shown in Table 18.1 has often helped supervisors and managers out of a difficult spot by suggesting a new approach.

Table 18.1 Decision making: notes for generating alternative courses of action

Questions	Notes
1. Have I done this sort of thing before? How?	
2. Could I do this in some other way?	
3. How did other people tackle it?	
4. What kind of people am I dealing with?	
5. How can this situation be changed to fit us?	
6. How can we adapt to fit this situation?	
7. How about using more? All of it? One? Two? Several? Less than we have done? Only a portion?	
8. How about using something else? Older? Newer? More expensive? Cheaper?	
9. How near?	
10. How far?	
11. In what direction?	
12. Could I do this in combination? With whom? With what?	
13. What about doing the opposite?	
14. What would happen if I did nothing?	
15. What specialist advice is available within the organization?	
16. What external bodies could give advice?	
17. What do subordinates, colleagues, superiors, suggest?	

Questions	×✓	Notes
18. Does company policy suggest any particular approach?		
19. Do the usual constraints really apply in this case?		

Table 18.2 Checklist on initiative

Questions	×✓	Notes
1. Do you anticipate bottlenecks and take steps to eliminate them?		
2. Do you keep abreast of changes in methods, materials and machinery, and are you able to discuss them with your superior?		
3. Have you checked that there are no longstanding anomalies in your department? If there are, have you a plan for eliminating them?		
4. Do you take advantage of any useful training which is available?		
5. Do you acknowledge scope for improvement in your department and take steps to achieve it?		
6. Do you think out alternative solutions to put to your superior when you do not yourself have the authority to take action on problems?		
7. Do you ensure that action taken is not wasted through lack of follow-up?		
8. Can you be relied upon to see problems through within the scope of your job, regardless of most obstacles?		

NB   Using initiative does not mean acting without authority

Questions

1. What is meant by completed staffwork and how is it likely to benefit
   (a) the boss,
   (b) the employee who does it?
2. Do you think completed staffwork is more appropriate when the manager is a team leader or specialist in his own field or when he is a general manager controlling diversely skilled specialists who know more about their respective professions or trades than he himself does? Give your reasons.

19. *Employee counselling*

During the course of your day's work you naturally compliment people on doing a good job or tactfully put them on the right lines when they have made mistakes. This on-the-spot guidance keeps the work ticking over properly, but does not always let employees know where they stand.

It would be quite a shock to many people if they knew what their boss thought of them. Assuming that no news is good news they carry on in their usual routine way until perhaps they see somebody else achieve a coveted promotion or be singled out for a special job, and then the truth strikes home hard. Often it is too late to do anything about it, so employees become bitter and antagonistic, or swear never to put themselves out again, doing only just enough to get by.

It is a good idea to have a regular six-monthly or yearly chat with each member of the team, standing back a bit from the day-to-day job and reviewing overall progress. If your kind of work goes in cycles, or is seasonal, or involves projects lasting several months, your chat can be timed accordingly. These reviews give you the following benefits:

- You acknowledge employees' successes, and they will be motivated to try harder.
- You all identify problem areas (such as poor liaison, shortages, backlogs, wasted work) and can jointly plan ways of solving these difficulties.
- You identify training needs and can plan how to arrange the necessary tuition or help them to help themselves with private study or practice.

- You discuss their future and can go some way towards reconciling their ambitions with their potential and the opportunities available. If these cannot be reconciled, at least you know you have the seeds of a problem there.
- You help them to sort out the priorities within their jobs, so that they will concentrate their efforts where they are most needed.

When you do this, don't get personal. It is probably better not to use the term 'employee appraisal', but call it something like 'job review'. Concentrate on talking about employees' performance, not their character. It is damaging to harm people's self-esteem by criticizing shortcomings over which they have no control, but you can criticize the score without humiliating the player. The key to successful staff counselling is to bear in mind the employee's needs, as shown on the scroll in Fig. 19.1.

How do you decide what you expect from an employee?

Sometimes this is laid down for you, or determined by work study, or perhaps there is a well established standard which everybody accepts in your industry. Beware that you are not stuck with an outdated and easily achieved level of performance which may have been satisfactory 10 years ago under different circumstances.

If there are no existing standards worth speaking of consult your boss and then decide what your aim should be. Then discuss with your team, individually or as a group, how these goals can be achieved. Tell them what you want from each of them and ask them what they need from you in order to score. If you set the right atmosphere they will respect you for this. I once firmly believed that no training officer should attempt to spend more than one week in four conducting courses until somebody showed me otherwise and then I enjoyed the new tempo. But keep a close watch on them for signs of strain.

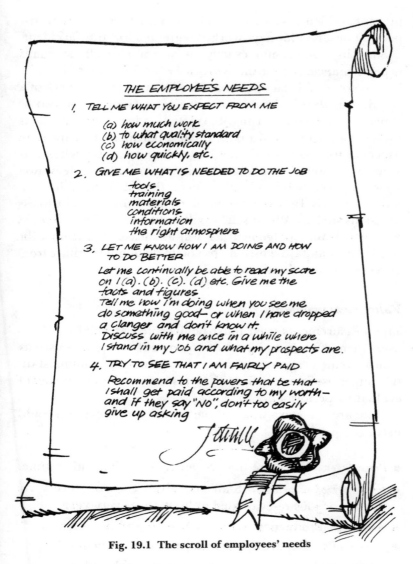

THE EMPLOYEE'S NEEDS

1. TELL ME WHAT YOU EXPECT FROM ME
   (a) how much work
   (b) to what quality standard
   (c) how economically
   (d) how quickly, etc.

2. GIVE ME WHAT IS NEEDED TO DO THE JOB
   tools
   training
   materials
   conditions
   information
   the right atmosphere

3. LET ME KNOW HOW I AM DOING AND HOW TO DO BETTER
   Let me continually be able to read my score on 1 (a). (b). (c). (d) etc. Give me the facts and figures
   Tell me how I'm doing when you see me do something good— or when I have dropped a clanger and don't know it.
   Discuss with me once in a while where I stand in my job and what my prospects are.

4. TRY TO SEE THAT I AM FAIRLY PAID
   Recommend to the powers that be that I shall get paid according to my worth— and if they say "No", don't too easily give up asking

Fig. 19.1 The scroll of employees' needs

Wherever possible you should try to *measure* performance so that there is a figure, percentage or ratio to go by. This makes it easier for people to see what they are doing. Instead of just asking people to work faster, improve quality, reduce costs or prevent accidents, you set a production quota, reject rate, cost per unit or target for days worked without a lost time accident.

Sometimes you cannot exactly measure a particular standard of performance, such as the skill of a welfare officer for example, but do not let this fact put you off. The main requirement of a standard is that it should mean the same thing to the two or three people who are using it. While it is better to have facts rather than opinions, if a boss and a subordinate looking at an aspect of the work ask themselves: 'How do we tell when it is being well done?' and after discussion arrive at a definition which is meaningful to both of them, then that definition is a valid standard. In making some of the most important business decisions such as 'Will it sell?' 'Will he fit into the job?' 'Should we trust them?', judgement as well as measurement must be used. Any standard which helps you to distinguish failure from success is better than none at all.

Valid measurements

The measurements used must be accepted as valid by those using them. For example, if the frequency of accidents is used as a measurement of a supervisor's effectiveness in training staff, that supervisor must believe that this is a valid and fair way of evaluating performance.

Here are some examples of the sort of yardsticks you could use:

- *Percentages*　Not more than X per cent machine down-time.
- *Frequency of occurrence*　Staff appraisals are done every six months or jobs re-evaluated at least once every year.
- *Averages*　Production averages X thousand per week.
- *Time limits*　Departmental budgets are ready before 1 April.
- *Absolute prohibition*　No employee starts work without receiving a lecture on safety.
- *Reference to external standards (legislation, etc.)*　The quality meets British Standards Institute specifications.

Should we measure only outputs?

It is obviously preferable to use as a standard the end *result* or output of the job. For example, in assessing a motorist's performance, you would look at his record of accidents and motoring convictions. But a Ministry of Transport learner driver examiner has to base his judgements largely on 'inputs': 'Does the candidate know his Highway Code?', and so on.

If you cannot define any good output standards, do not be reluctant to define the input, i.e., a prescribed way of working known to give effective results. For example, you might specify as one of the standards of effective recruitment the requirement that aptitude tests are used.

Why write down standards?

Standards are of greater value if they are recorded as a reminder. The piece of paper must be seen as a tool, not as an end in itself.

When you have agreed what you want your team to do, and how you will be able to tell when they are on target, you must listen to what your staff say they want from you in order to do what is expected of them. This takes care of the second point on the scroll.

Point 3 is partly achieved by ensuring that employees can always read their score card, by giving them guidance on a day-to-day basis as needed, and doing your six-monthly or yearly review.

The six-monthly or yearly job review interview

Before you ask an employee to discuss this with you, let her know well in advance so that she can prepare for it. You could give her the following questions to think about for a week beforehand, in order to help her collect her thoughts:

- What have you accomplished during the period?
- Are there any changes which you would wish to see that will help you to accomplish more in the forthcoming year?
- Do you think you have complete understanding of the requirements of your job?

Employee counselling 233

- Are there any aspects of the job which are vague?
- Which parts of your job do you do best?
- Which parts of the job are you not quite happy about?
- Do you think you have skills and aptitudes which are not fully used in your present job?
- What training do you think would help you to improve your performance in your present job?

Choose the right time for the interview

Make sure that the employee is in a receptive mood, not tired and touchy. Just prior to the job review, make the following preparations:

1. Set aside an hour.
2. Choose a suitable place. Don't talk across a table or desk as this can create a barrier.
3. Ensure against interruptions by telephone or visitors.

Prepare thoroughly

Read in advance, and keep at hand:
1. The employee's personal history sheet, file or record card.
2. A summary of the training received.
3. A note of any targets attempted during the period under review.
4. A note of success, or lack of it, in attaining these.

Consider:

1. What the individual has been up against (e.g., problems with work pressure, material shortages, equipment, etc.).
2. What work has had to be pulled in over and above the normal work routine.

A four-point plan

Use the plan shown in Table 19.1 as a guide.

Listen more than you talk   The chapter on selecting staff gives some advice on encouraging interviewees to speak up for

Table 19.1

1. Ask the employee what he or she feels have been the year's achievements in the job.	2. Ask what the main problems were. If you can see a problem which he or she has not recognized, mention it and ask for suggestions. Tactfully contribute yours.
3. Discuss together the next year's targets.	4. Discuss what help is needed, including any training requirements.

themselves. By listening you can check whether the person has a clear idea of the work to be done and the priorities involved. If the individual is hazy about this you can guide him or her towards a better understanding of these matters. The secret of encouraging people to talk is in asking the right kind of questions.

Ask open questions   Don't ask leading questions, that is, ones which imply the answer by the way it is phrased. Leading questions always carry an assumption, such as 'I take it . . .' 'I suppose . . .' 'Presumably . . .' 'No doubt . . .' or '. . . , doesn't it?' So unless you are 200 per cent certain you are right, avoid such remarks as:

'I suppose you've had problems with your machine?'
'No doubt the trainee held you back a bit?'
'I suppose you wouldn't mind going over to shift work?'

Reflect   When a person makes a comment show that you understand what he or she is getting at by putting their views back to them in your own words. This does not mean you are agreeing, and if you have to express a contrary opinion you can do so later, but it makes sense to encourage the individual to express his or her feelings fully so that you really understand what it is that you are disagreeing with.

This is the technique mentioned in Chapter 7 on grievance interviewing.

Here is an example of how the interview might work out:

BOB (*the manager*): Hullo Jack, come in and take a seat. Coffee?

JACK: Hullo Bob, thanks.

BOB: Did you have a chance to think about the questions I gave you the other day? You know, the ones about this progress report?

JACK: Yes, where shall we start?

BOB: Let's start with what you've achieved during the last six months. Is there anything you would especially single out?

JACK: I suppose it was something just to keep up production, especially during February with all the power problems.

BOB (*responding to Jack's mood*): That took some doing.

JACK: You know, I think the firm should buy its own generator.

BOB (*although Bob has his doubts, he doesn't turn down Jack's idea but reflects it neutrally, to encourage further comment*): You feel a generator would help?

JACK: Yes, that would get us out of some of the real trouble we hit mid-February with the Thompson order. That set us back £10 000.

BOB: I'll make a note of that suggestion, Jack. Can't promise anything, but it's worth thinking about. What else would you feel was outstanding about the last six months?

JACK: Well, Bob, I think I made out pretty well during the week you were away at the European exhibition and I deputized for you.

BOB: You feel the week went pretty smoothly.

JACK: I had my worries of course.

BOB: What were the main ones?

JACK: They asked me some tricky questions about the quality standards and I felt I would have done better if I had a better knowledge of inspection.

BOB: You would like a bit of training in that. Any particular point you need to know about?

(Jack was fairly pleased with himself about the week's deputizing. Bob, the manager, was pleased with the way he had held the fort, but knew that there were a few problems. However, he refrains from deflating Jack, but gets him to appreciate his own shortcomings, and to recognize that he needs training. The secret is in reflecting, showing EMPATHY, tuning in to his mood, and letting him discover things about himself by considering the right questions.)

No surprises   There should be such good regular day-to-day and week-to-week communication between you and each member of your team that very little comes as a surprise during the job review. For example, if it came out in this chat that you thought the quality of someone's work was below average and he or she had been under the impression that their work was good, you would know that in future more frequent guidance was needed.

Although comments in these reviews should be more or less as anticipated, such interviews are well worth while as they permit you both to take an overall view.

View the whole period, not just recent events   A bad mistake made last week should not distort your assessment over the year as a whole.

References to other employees and their work   When discussing X's work with him or her, don't compare it favourably or unfavourably with Y's. Word always gets back to the person criticized and either way it tends to undermine relationships.

Summarize at the end   Recap on the main points, especially the action you are each going to take, and then end the chat on an encouraging note.

If you don't think people can take it, don't give it   If you know that criticism—even constructively given—would only make matters worse, avoid giving it. Let them do all the talking. Common sense must prevail for all formal systems; and if the system says you have got to appraise every employee, keep it short and sweet in cases like this.

Besides the employee counselling interview which you would probably set up on a regular six-monthly or yearly basis, many other opportunities will occur for listening to employees and nipping serious problems in the bud.

One of these opportunities is the sickness self-certification interview

Doctors do not issue sickness certificates for the first seven days of absence from work. Instead, employees fill in and sign their own certification forms.

Whether the sickness is physical, psychological, imagined, or invented to give the malingerer time off, you know that there is a problem. If you handle the return to work interview well you will have a good chance of finding out what that problem is.

1. Make sure you keep the necessary absence records, and consult them first.
2. Interview the employee in private as soon as possible on returning to work.
3. Make sure that the self-certification form is completed by the employee in front of you in company time at that interview.
4. Use all your interviewing and counselling skills. If the person is malingering perhaps there is something which could be put right in the working environment (favouritism, discrimination frustration, working conditions)?

5. Use tact and diplomacy. Beware about asking intimate medical questions.
6. Offer positive suggestions and help if needed.
7. Monitor the employee's performance and condition. Follow up to ensure that the problem(s) is being resolved.

Table 19.2 Checklist on counselling

Questions	×√	Notes
1. Do you have a six-monthly talk with each of your employees about their progress at work?		
2. Do you let them know a week in advance so that they can prepare themselves?		
3. Do you prepare yourself by having their records available, especially any notes about their achievements or problems?		
4. Do you plan what you are going to tell them and ask them?		
5. Do you set aside an hour for the interview?		
6. Do you organize a comfortable room with no desk to act as a barrier?		
7. Do you ensure against telephone/visitor interruptions?		
8. When you conduct this interview do you listen twice as much as you talk?		
9. During the interview do you (a) ask open questions? (b) reflect?		
10. Do you summarize what has been discussed and recap on the points for action?		
11. Do you make good use of the return to work interview under the new self-certification rules?		

Questions

1. Do you think job review discussions are useful? Please give your reasons.
2. What preparations should you make before the interview?
3. What do you think are the important *do's* and *don'ts* to be observed when reviewing an individual's performance?
4. Some managers say that periodic counselling sessions are unnecessary because they are in close touch with their people all the time. How would you answer this line of reasoning?
5. Outline how you would conduct a return to work interview after a person has been off sick?
6. Besides the self-certification interview, what other circumstances might call for counselling?

20. *Supervision in the office*

No industrial or commercial undertaking can operate without office activity. Office workers are employed in the public sector, in manufacturing companies, in service industries and in commercial organizations. Their tasks cover a wide range of activities; reception, switchboard, typing, dealing with enquiries, documentation, book-keeping, computing and operating a rapidly increasing variety of electronic equipment. As soon as you are given responsibility for the work of another member of staff you are taking on the function of an office supervisor, even if you are not given that title, and you should be aware of the ingredients of successful office supervision.

Three essentials in office supervision are:

- to bear in mind at all times the objectives of the whole organization;
- to see clearly how your section contributes to these;
- to understand fully how it inter-relates with other sections and departments.

Office supervisors, more than any other kind, need to keep these essentials constantly in mind because of the sometimes intangible output of clerical work. By communicating them to your team and reminding your staff about them, you let everybody know that they are doing a worthwhile job which is essential to the smooth operation of the whole organization. Teamwork within the section and liaison with other units are always key areas of your job and both topics are dealt with in other chapters.

The office supervisor

A typical office supervisor is responsible for the work of about six other people who each have a different function, and probably has an operational workload which usually takes up about half the working hours. If you find that your own workload prevents you from giving enough time to the supervisory aspects of the job, you should take this up with your manager and evolve a plan for redistributing the work.

Any organization, big or small, looks to its office supervisors to achieve maximum use of resources: people, space, equipment, time, money, systems and procedures. However advanced or sophisticated your other resources may be, the human one is still that which will make the greatest contribution to the success of the enterprise or, conversely, hold it back. So we will begin with this aspect.

Choosing the right people

When staff are recruited for your section you should always be involved because you know what ingredients are necessary to build an effective team. You must look for people with flexible and adaptable attitudes in order that they can cope with the changing technology. Don't rule out older people with valuable experience—you *can* teach an old dog new tricks but it does take a little longer! Refer to Chapter 3 on staff selection.

Training them

Chapter 5 deals with staff training, but for the office employee it is particularly useful to produce a training analysis and programme, especially when introducing new technology or training beginners. Table 20.1 shows one for an order clerk. The *main duties* are the important jobs to be done by the person concerned, while the *tasks* are a more detailed specification of what each duty involves. The other two columns in the table specify the knowhow needed and the means by which it should be acquired.

When the trainee is asssigned to an 'instructor' (who could be a supervisor, section head, or an experienced clerk) it is

Table 20.1 Training analysis and program (Position: order clerk)

Main duties	Tasks	Skills/knowledge required	Normal programme (tutor and duration)	
1. Take telephone orders	Record particulars	Effective telephone communication	Training dept	1 day (standard course)
	Advise customer about delivery	Special customers	Supervisor	1 day
		Products	Sales dept	½ day
		Availability	Supervisor	1 day
		Discounts	Stores	1 day
		Freighting or delivery method	Shipping dept	½ day
	Process the order	Computer basics	Section head	3 days

2. Maintain stock levels	Maintain stock-control records	Computerized system	Stores	2 days
	Order when necessary	Minimum stock levels	Supervisor	½ day
		Discounts for quantity	Section head	1 day
		Alternative suppliers	Purchasing dept	2 days
		Alternative products	Supervisor	1 day

important that the instructor should be given the required time to do it properly. Here is a good formula to follow:

Preparation   The day before the trainee arrives the instructor considers what the trainee knows already and then prepares papers and documents, equipment, and a session plan (the order and priority of points to make) accordingly.

Step 1   The instructor puts the trainee at ease and creates a desire to learn by letting him or her know that what he or she is about to do will benefit both the trainee and the company. It is important to explain at this stage where the job fits in to the overall scheme of things. By putting the task into its proper context the instructor will enlist the trainee's brain—not just his or her memory!

Step 2   The instructor does the job, explaining what he or she is doing as the job progresses. The trainee observes and asks questions.

Step 3   The trainee does the job and the instructor monitors him or her, guiding over the difficulties, answering questions and giving encouragement.

Step 4   The instructor sits nearby but gets on with his or her own work, remaining available for reference when difficulties or problems arise and again giving encouragement.

Step 5   The work goes direct to the trainee. The instructor no longer sits alongside, but checks the work at the end of the day. The instructor observes and encourages.

Step 6   The instructor lets the trainee know that he or she has made the grade, and praises the trainee's efforts.

At the start of the training the instructor has all the knowledge and skill and the trainee has none. Figure 20.1 shows how the skill or knowledge is progressively transferred from the trainer to the trainee.

Preparation
is the key to success!

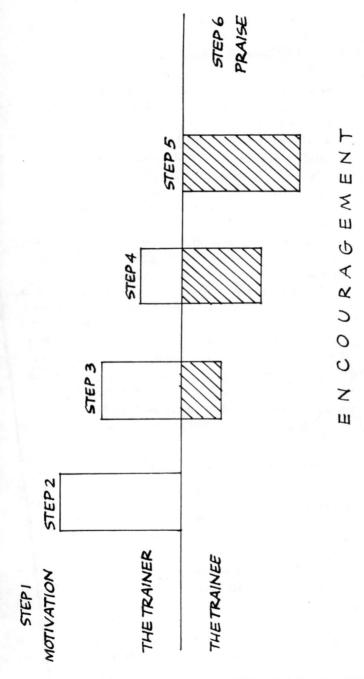

Figure 20.1 Six steps in at-the-desk training

Looking after health and safety

The well laid-out and tidy office which looks efficient is more likely to meet health and safety requirements than an untidy one. Even in factories more accidents are caused by falls, bumping into and tripping over objects, than are caused by machinery. All these things can and do happen in offices and so do fires and electrical hazards. In addition, offices have their own special pitfalls such as guillotines, kettles, trailing flexes and inflammable correcting fluids. Under the Health and Safety at Work Act 1974 you, as supervisor, are responsible for seeing that your team use safe working practices; your employers are reponsible for providing appropriate instruction and training in health and safety. You should be constantly vigilant about health and safety matters and report faults promptly. The amount of electrical and electronic equipment in offices is increasing rapidly but paperwork is not totally eliminated, resulting in increased hazards. Liquids and electricity do not mix, nor do cigarettes and wastepaper bins. More equipment calls for improved ventilation to combat the heat generated— smoking may have to be banned except during rest breaks. Read the chapter on safety carefully and note the hazards which can occur in any kind of workplace; make a list of the hazards which occur in offices which are not found in production areas.

Health and safety in the electronic office

It is vital that office systems keep up with the increasing demands being placed upon them by the speed of today's transactions and requirements for information and data on which your organization depends for its survival and success. Later in this chapter we examine the introduction of electronic data processing in more detail but this section deals with the health and safety aspects involved.

An integral part of your computer system will be the visual display unit (VDU) and this could in certain circumstances cause health hazards. As well as attention to lighting levels you will need to look at noise levels, ventilation, posture, and reduction of sources of glare. The Health and Safety Executive *Report on Visual Display Units* published by HMSO in 1983 gives useful guidance on these matters and also deals with rest pauses. Short, frequently occurring rest pauses (away from the VDU) are more beneficial than longer ones taken less often. Rest pauses should be arranged prior to the onset of fatigue— not as a recuperative period.

If you supervise VDU operators you should keep up to date with all publications on hazards. These can be obtained from the Health and Safety Executive, the equipment manufacturers and 'white-collar' unions. Other workers who are not classed as VDU operators will be using these installations intermittently, and you should monitor the length of time such workers spend on them and see that the same provisions for rest pauses are made. One piece of research showed clearly that the incidence and areas of recorded aches and pains developed progressively during the transition from office worker to typist, part-time VDU operator and then full-time VDU operator.

It is important to take any such complaints seriously and to see that they are treated early by rest from the operation. Explore the possibilities of job rotation as a solution to this problem. Tenosynovitis (repetitive strain injury of muscles and tendons in the fingers) is an example of a condition which is simple to treat in the early stages but painful and even crippling later on. Prevention is better than cure and it is clearly the office supervisor's responsibility to see that the correct steps are taken to prevent repetitive strain injury.

Helpful booklets for office supervisors can be obtained from HM Stationery Office and from the Royal Society for the Prevention of Accidents. (ROSPA, Canon House, The Priory, Queensway, Birmingham B4 6BS. Tel. 021-223-2461).

Involving staff in securing economy, efficiency and effectiveness

As new technology becomes universal it will present increasing opportunities for evaluating existing procedures and devising new methods. 'Value for money' is the term which one local authority uses to describe its strategy for facing the challenge of providing increased services from limited resources.

Use the following definitions to assess your office on a *value for money* basis:

- *Inputs* resources available, e.g. staff, equipment.
- *Activities* what is actually being done, e.g. preparation and distribution of documents and information.
- *Outputs* results of activities, e.g. products or services completed and invoiced.
- EFFICIENCY is the relationship between *inputs* and *activities* but EFFECTIVENESS is the relationship between *activities* and *outputs*.

You could have a very busy *efficient* office where considerable paperwork is completed or data distributed electronically but which is not *effective* in terms of results achieved. Most experienced office staff can cite examples of this and as supervisor you should ensure that your section is not operating on these lines. Try asking each member of your team what they think is the purpose of each task they undertake. You may get some surprising answers! Make it clear that they are accountable for *results which benefit the company*, not just activity, and discuss with them how best to achieve those results. When the ideas have been contributed and evaluated, adopt the best ones and do not hesitate to go to your manager with those that require his approval. Make sure that the originator of the idea receives the credit, and let those who came up with other suggestions know why they weren't being adopted (perhaps *yet*). They must be left feeling that they will always be *involved*.

Information technology

Centrally stored information, rapid retrieval of data, word processing, document distribution, electronic mailing: the futuristic concept of the integrated electronic office is now a reality, the only constraint on any organization being availability of capital to invest and the ability to justify such investment. This means that the methods by which office work is carried out are changing rapidly as a result of the introduction of electronic methods of processing office work. Such methods are now generally referred to as *information technology* (IT) and can dramatically improve efficiency if applied in the right way. Problems arise when a computer is installed without a realistic analysis of the expected results; be sure you are going to be able to get the right *software* (the programming) before considerable sums are spent on *hardware* (the equipment).

The computer should help you to process work more speedily, more accurately, or over a wider distribution. You and your team would benefit from a short session of computerization awareness training right at the outset, so that you all understand the full potential of any installation and develop a positive attitude towards its use. Automated office systems are not an aid to traditional ways of working—they actually replace traditional approaches to office work; as a result, large-scale reorganization of office work is now possible.

The effect on office workers should be to reduce tedious tasks and release them for more interesting work. You must see that this is what happens in practice, otherwise staff will be reduced to repetitive button-pushing with consequent detrimental effects on morale. Be receptive to ideas from your team about which tasks they would like to see computerized and in this way you can secure their commitment to the successful operation of any new system.

This commitment is vital. Existing staff who are accustomed to the visual and physical reassurance of holding a paper file in their hands will require considerable help in re-thinking attitudes in order to work effectively with electronic files and screen-to-screen communication now possible between departments, companies or even countries. Here are some guidelines to help you introduce the changes involved.

Guidelines for introducing information technology

1. Read the chapter on introducing change.
2. Interview your team members individually to explore their fears and expectations of the proposed system.
3. Note all potential problems, e.g., lighting, eyesight.
4. Call a team meeting to ventilate concerns.
5. Report to your manager and seek expert advice on the feasibility of your team's ideas (management will probably have nominated a senior coordinator for the installation).
6. Obtain all possible information from higher management, health and safety sources and the equipment manufacturers. Get yourself really well informed so that you can answer questions.
7. Brief your team about the time scale for introduction of the new technology and the training arrangements. Be honest with them about the amount of work involved in programming information currently held in traditional record-keeping systems.
8. Ensure that management provide you with the necessary 'hand-holding' resource during programming.
9. Liaise with other departments who will be affected during the changeover and when the new equipment is in operation.
10. Monitor the health and well-being of your team during and after installation and report all problems to your manager, with your suggestions for resolving them.
11. Make sure the system is used to its full potential.
12. Familiarize yourself with the provisions and implications of the Data Protection Act 1984.

The above guidelines will help you develop the right attitudes in your existing team. You should feel confident and enthusiastic about the installation yourself and basically 'make them love it'. When recruiting new staff seek people who are mature, responsible, systematic and more self-reliant than traditional office workers were expected to be. Remember that they, and your existing team, will each be communicating on their own directly with a word processor or computer and will not be in conventional work groups where small problems can be shared with adjacent clerks.

Self development for office supervisors

Self development is the process by which a person:

- identifies personal development goals;
- takes responsibility for an action plan to reach those goals;
- develops methods of monitoring progress;
- re-assesses goals periodically in the light of experience.

People who know what they want and set about securing it always seem to do better than those who are unsure of their objectives, even if the latter have been exposed to greater opportunities. The steps shown in Table 20.2 will ensure that you are in the first category:

Table 20.2 Action plan for self-development

Take advantage of training opportunities in your own organization.	See your training officer.
Seek out books in your local library.	
Read relevant magazines.	
Find out about courses at local adult education centres, technical colleges and colleges of further education.	e.g., Business Education Council OND or HND in Business Studies; National Examination Board for Supervisory Studies with special options for office supervisors.
Ask at above centres about Open Access Learning Centres.	This is studying at your own pace and at times to suit, with tutorial support.
Consider Distance Learning (short courses available).	Details from the Open University, Open Business School, Milton Keynes.

While books are essential for in-depth study, magazines are particularly useful for keeping up to date. The implications of office technology are developing so rapidly at present that even the most thorough book could contain out-of-date information quite quickly. At the time of writing there are around twenty magazines on office equipment and systems, so look around for the one most closely related to your field of work.

In conclusion

As an office supervisor you will be working very closely with, and in, your team and this may present difficulties, especially if you were promoted from within. You can afford to adopt a relaxed attitude and be close to your staff when discussing matters of mutual interest during breaks, on company outings or other social occasions like birthdays, but make sure that the standards you expect are clearly spelled out and any deviation from them is dealt with promptly. An outsider visiting an organization recently commented on the pleasant informal manner of an office supervisor and received the reply from a team member, 'Yes, she's very easy-going so long as everything is done instantly and perfectly!' How would you feel if this comment had been make about your supervisory style?

You should now proceed to read the other chapters in this book . . .

Questions

1. How would you set about assessing the potential for automation (or increased automation) in your section?
2. How do the health hazards of VDUs compare with those of typewriters and photocopiers?
3. How would you vary the guidelines for introducing information technology for use in your own section?
4. What are the health and safety hazards in your office?
5. Is your section efficient *and* effective?
6. What steps are you taking for self-development?
7. What do you know about 'white-collar' unions (e.g. NALGO, ASTMS, APEX and also special sections of manual unions)?

Table 20.3   Checklist on office efficiency

Questions	×✓	Notes
1. Do all members of the team know clearly what their job is and what standards are expected?		
2. Have all members of staff been given sufficient authority to enable them to carry out their duties effectively? Are they ready to be given more authority?		
3. Have you analysed the quantity and quality of work being produced?		
4. Do your experienced staff know how to instruct?		
5. Are you bringing along the younger members of the team?		
6. Are the capabilities of staff being fully used?		
7. Does your office layout result in unnecessary movement?		
8. Is there sufficient equipment or is there a time loss during sharing and waiting?		
9. Do you regularly critically examine your systems and methods?		
10. Are you keeping unnecessary records?		
11. How often do delays occur due to lost or misplaced records?		
12. Have you checked the distribution, state and accessibility of manuals and instructions?		
13. What longer-term remedies are necessary to prevent a recurrence of any backlogs?		
14. Are certain individuals doing more than their fair share of work?		
15. Are the majority of errors being made by a few individuals?		

Index

ACAS, xi
Accident prevention, 123–127
Accident-prone employees, 131
Accounting terms, 192–195
Appreciation, 8
Art of listening, 82–86
Authority and responsibility,
   103–105, 152

Board of directors, 157
Brainstorming, 188
Breakeven, 195
Breaking jobs into steps, 62, 63
Budgetary control, 180, 181
Buzz groups, 77

Change, introducing, 89–97
Clerical staff, 241–245
Committee assignments, 56
Communication, 113–122
Complaints, 81–88
Completed staff work, 223, 224
Computers, 248–250
Consultation, 11
Cost accountant's role, 182
Cost accounting terms, 192–195
Cost reduction, 180–199
Counselling, 229–239
Creative thinking, 225
Critical path, 215, 216

Daily contact, 116
Daily goal planning sheet, 207
D-day minus principle, 215
De Bono, Edward, 225
Delegation, 55, 146–155
Deputy, your, 54–58

Dinosaur Ltd, 113
Direct costs:
   labour, 192
   material, 193
Discipline, 99–111

Effectiveness in offices, 248
Efficiency in offices, 248
Electronic office, 246
Empathy, 237
Employee specification, 27–29
Employment interview, 29–37
Example, 125

Fatigue, 185
Five rules for grievance
   interviews, 84–86
Fixed indirect overheads, 193
Forgetting, 64
Frustration, 19
Functional supervision, 159

Grievance procedure, 86, 87
Grievances, 81–88
Groups, 9–11
Group instruction, 77–80
Group training techniques, 71–80
Guided experience, 56

Health and safety, 123–137, 246
Herzberg, F., 6
Hierarchy of needs, Maslow, 170
Human relations, 1–26

Indirect costs:
   labour, 193
   material, 193

Individual employee training schedule, 65–67
Individual training needs analysis, 65, 66
Induction, 42–49
Information technology, 248–250
Initiative, 223–228
Injuries, 123–137
Inspection schedule, 211
Instruction, 59–64
Interviews:
  counselling, 229–240
  disciplinary, 99–111
  employment, 29, 34–37
  grievance, 81–88
Introducing new employees, 42–49
Investigating accidents, 129
Involvement, 178

Job enrichment, 20–24
Job review interviews, 233–238
Job rotation, 57
Job specification, 30, 32

Key results areas, 201

Labour costs, 192
Larks and owls, 210
Lateral thinking, 225
Law, your job, and the, xi
'Law of the situation', 108–109
Leadership, 1–18
Leading questions, 36
Learning plateau, 60
Lecture, 75–77
Liability, legal, 123
Liaison, interdepartmental, 166–172
Line organization, 158

McGregor, Douglas, 21
Machine downtime, 189, 190
Management by exception, 153
Managing director, 157
Managing time, 200–222
Maslow, Abraham, 170
Material costs, 193
Matrix management, 164

Measurements of performance, 231–233
Methods improvement, 174–179
Monotony, 20–24
Morning inspection, 217
Motivation, 1–18
Must know, should know, nice to know, 46

National Certificate/Diploma in Business Studies, 251
National Examinations Board for Supervisory Studies, 52, 251
Nerves, 71, 72
Nervous tension, 25–26
New employees, 42–49

Office employees, 241–253
Older employees, 130, 189–192
Open questions, 235
Organization, principles of, 156–173
Overhead costs, 193

Pending jobs list, 204
PERT, 215, 216
Philips Gloeilampenfabrieken, 20
Planning, 200–222
Potential hazards, 125
Preventive and contingency plans, 225
Productivity, 182
Project teams, 164
Project work, 56

Quality circles, 178, 179
Questioning technique, 177
Questions in interviews, 36, 235

Recapitulation, 79
Recovery of overheads, 194
References, 38–40
Reflecting, 235–237
Reprimands, 105–109
Resistance to change, 89–97
Responsibility, 103–105, 152
Restrictive practices, 4, 143
Rework, 191

Role conflict, 169
Rush job, 218

Safety, 123–137
Safety representatives, 132
Scrap, 191
Scroll, 231
Section training plan, 68
Selecting staff, 27–41
Self certification (sickness), 238
Self development, 50–53
    office supervisor, 251, 252
Shareholders, 157
Shop stewards, 139–145
Span of control, 161
'Staff' and 'line' organization, 159
Standard costing, 194
Standards, 230–233
Subordinate supervisors,
    training, 54–58
Suggestions, 120
Supervisory training, 52–58
Suspension without pay, 110

Targets, 6
Taylor, F. W., 158, 159
Teams, 8–10
Telephone reference, 38–40
Tests, 37

Theory X and Theory Y, 21
'Thermals' in interviews, 34, 35
Time log, 208
Time management, 200–222
Trade unions, 139–145
Training, 50–70
Training analysis for office
    staff, 243
Transition, school to work, 47

Understudying, 55
Union representative, 139–145
Urgent or important? 205–206

Value analysis, 187, 188
Variable indirect overheads, 193
VDUs, 246, 247

Waiting time, 190
Waste reduction, 184, 185
Work structuring, 20–24
Work methods, 174–179

X, Theory, 21

Y, Theory, 21
Year to view organizer, 211

Mountbatten Library

Tel: (01703) 319249 Fax: (01703) 319697
Please return this book on or before the last date stamped.
Loans may be renewed on application to the Library Staff.

ONE WEEK LOAN